William Warburton

Twayne's English Authors Series

Bertram H. Davis, Editor
Florida State University

TEAS 361

WILLIAM WARBURTON
(1698–1779)
*From the painting by William Hoare
in the Hurd Library, Hartlebury Castle
Photograph courtesy of the Bishop of Worcester*

William Warburton

By Robert M. Ryley
York College
City University of New York

Twayne Publishers • Boston

William Warburton

Robert M. Ryley

Copyright © 1984 by G. K. Hall & Company
All Rights Reserved
Published by Twayne Publishers
A Division of G. K. Hall & Company
70 Lincoln Street
Boston, Massachusetts 02111

Book Production by Marne B. Sultz

Book Design by Barbara Anderson

Printed on permanent/durable acid-free
paper and bound in the United States of
America.

Library of Congress Cataloging in Publication Data

Ryley, Robert M.
  William Warburton.

  (Twayne's English authors series : TEAS 361)
  Includes bibliographical references and index.
  1. Warburton, William, Bp. of Gloucester, 1698–1779—
Criticism and interpretation.   I. Title.   II. Series.
PR3757.W7R94   1984   230'.3'0924   83–22686
ISBN 0–8057–6847–5

For Alison

Contents

About the Author

Robert M. Ryley was educated at Colby College, the University of Massachusetts, and the University of Minnesota. He has taught English at Queens College and is a charter member of the faculty of York College of the City University of New York. His articles and reviews have appeared in *Philological Quarterly, Papers on Language and Literature, Studies in the Literary Imagination, College English, Transactions of the Cambridge Bibliographical Society, American Book Collector,* and the *Armchair Detective.* He is currently working on a study of the American poet and novelist Kenneth Fearing.

Preface

For almost fifteen years I have been trying to buy a secondhand copy of the standard biography of William Warburton, A. W. Evans's long-out-of-print *Warburton and the Warburtonians*. That it has been easier to write my own book on Warburton suggests one reason for its being: to provide an accessible source of information about the now-obscure figure who, at the height of his fame in the middle of the eighteenth century, was among the most eminent theologians, scholars, and critics in all of Europe.

Unlike Evans's book, however, this is not a biography. The Chronology and the list of primary sources in the Bibliography provide the essential facts of Warburton's life and literary career, and chapter 1 is a study of his character, but the body of the book is organized topically around his major intellectual pursuits. Despite necessary duplication, it complements Evans by treating in detail topics that he had to slight owing to the breadth of his coverage or to the unavailability of knowledge that only another half-century of scholarship would produce.

The book begins with an introduction to Warburton as a man. In no other writer, perhaps, have such potentially great powers of mind been so often trivialized or misdirected by moral and emotional weaknesses. Now that psychobiography has added yet another terror to death, he is probably fortunate that the known facts of his childhood are too meager to be tempting to Freudians. One known fact, however—that he was the eldest of the surviving Warburton children—suggested the possibility that studies of the effect of birth order on personality might be illuminating. To the extent that they are, I have drawn on some of them to advance tentative explanations of his eccentricities. In doing so I have tried to be as tactful as possible, keeping in mind the obvious truth that while birth-order theory may account for traits that he shares with many other first-born males, it will not account for the extreme form they take in him.[1]

Chapter 1 also considers the most important event of his life, his decision to defend the orthodoxy of Alexander Pope's *Essay on Man*. Because he is said to have attacked the poem when it first appeared and because his friendship with Pope advanced his ecclesiastical career and made him rich, his reputation has suffered from the widespread suspicion that he sacrificed principle to ambition. Chapter 1 examines in depth the theological, political, and emotional context in which the crucial decision was made.

Though intended as a general introduction to one aspect of Warburton's work, each of the next four chapters is based on research in heretofore-neglected primary sources and will, I hope, prove useful to professional scholars as well as to students. Chapter 2 confines itself to the three major theological works: *The Alliance between Church and State, Julian,* and *The Divine Legation of Moses,* including the posthumously published book 9, which, except for an early nineteenth-century prize essay by a Cambridge undergraduate,[2] has been largely ignored. Chapter 3 studies Warburton's theoretical, historical, and interpretive criticism, including the three critical essays in the *Divine Legation.* Chapter 4 examines the editions of Shakespeare and Pope. Because the former is rare and seldom found even in university libraries, I have described its contents in detail and quoted from it copiously. The more readily available edition of Pope I have treated more briefly, defending it, however, against the strictures of some recent scholars. After a brief analysis of Warburton's style, chapter 5 focuses on his personal letters. I have quoted at length from many of these, especially those that remain unpublished and were unknown to his earlier biographers. A heretofore unpublished letter to Sir Thomas Hanmer is printed in full. The final chapter contains a brief history of Warburton's reputation and concludes with a general estimate of his work.

A narrowly educated specialist of the twentieth century writing about a polymath of the eighteenth has to depend more than most other scholars on the assistance of friends and colleagues. I want to express tardy gratitude to the late Herbert Davis, who in a seminar at the University of Minnesota first stimulated my interest in Warburton by suggesting that the latter's much-maligned edition of Pope could be defended. I also owe thanks to Professor Robert E. Moore and to that most admirable of all eighteenth-century scholars, the late Professor Samuel Holt Monk, for encouraging the interest that Professor Davis began.

A number of people in England have made direct and indirect contributions to the writing of the book. Mr. A. J. Cook, district librarian in Newark-on-Trent, the city of Warburton's birth, twice consulted parish registers to establish the dates of birth and death of various members of the Warburton family. He also went to the trouble of asking the Lincoln County archivist to check the Brant Broughton burials register for the burial date of Warburton's mother.[3] The bishop of Worcester graciously permitted me to use the Hurd Library in Hartlebury Castle and to reproduce the library's portrait of Warburton as the frontispiece. Mr. L. W. Greenwood (whose grandfather once lived in the house where Warburton was born) kindly opened the library for me and located the books and manuscripts I needed. My former colleague Michael Seymour did everything possible to facilitate my research at the Bodleian Library.

Closer to home, the overworked staff of the York College Library has been consistently helpful, especially Mrs. Shirley Geffner, who, with infinite patience and good humor, raided the libraries of fifty states for books I requested through interlibrary loan. The Pierpont Morgan Library kindly granted permission to quote in full Warburton's letter to Sir Thomas Hanmer of 21 May 1739. Professor Anita Lasry of Vassar College helped me in important ways with the section in chapter 3 on the history of romance, and my colleague Professor Rainer Pineas, besides providing invaluable information and advice, contributed to the section on Shakespeare by listening while I ran on about it. My old friend Professor Keith Fort of Georgetown University supplied important information from the Folger Shakespeare Library. Another old friend, Professor Thomas B. Gilmore, Jr., of Georgia State University, and a new one, Professor Deborah Knuth of Colgate University, read several chapters in manuscript and caught a number of howlers and obscurities. Any remaining howlers and obscurities must be in the chapters that they did not see.

I am indebted most of all to my family. My sister, Mrs. Katherine R. Dow, has always encouraged me to use my head. At the age of six, in a London apartment near Holland Park, my son, Alex Ryley, helped me index many pages of notes; more recently he has helped me keep Warburton in perspective by asking, "What is that turkey's name again?" The numberless contributions of my wife, Alison M. Ryley, need not be mentioned, since she is the book's final cause.

Robert M. Ryley

York College
City University of New York

Chronology

1698   William Warburton born 24 December (old style) in Newark-on-Trent, Nottinghamshire, to George and Elizabeth Hobman Warburton.

1706   Father dies. Warburton sent briefly to Newark Free School, then to the Grammar School at Oakham, Rutlandshire.

1714   Returns to Newark Free School. Articled to John Kirke, attorney, in East Markham, Nottinghamshire.

1719–1722   Returns to Newark. Practices law. Assists cousin as schoolmaster. Holds office of town clerk jointly with Richard Twells.

1723   *Miscellaneous Translations in Prose and Verse.* 22 December, ordained deacon.

1727   1 March, ordained priest. Presented living of Greasley, Nottinghamshire. *A Critical and Philosophical Enquiry into the Causes of Prodigies and Miracles. Legal Judicature in Chancery Stated.*

1728   Resigns Greasley for rectory of Brant Broughton, Lincolnshire. Made Master of Arts upon first visit of George II to Cambridge.

1729   Begins correspondence on Shakespeare with Lewis Theobald. Publishes three anonymous attacks on Pope in the *Daily Journal.*

1730   Presented combined livings of Frisby and Great Steeping, Leicestershire, which he holds *in absentia* until 1756.

1731   Begins *Divine Legation of Moses.*

1733   *A Defense of Sir Robert Sutton.*

1734   Theobald's Shakespeare, with many notes and portions of the preface by Warburton.

1735   Begins correspondence on Shakespeare with Sir Thomas Hanmer.

1736   Breaks with Theobald. *The Alliance between Church and State.*

1738   *Divine Legation*, vol. 1. *Vindication of the Author of the Divine Legation. Faith Working by Charity* (sermon). First letter on Pope's *Essay on Man.*

1739   More letters on the *Essay on Man*. Begins correspondence with Pope. Breaks with Hanmer. *A Vindication of Mr. Pope's Essay on Man* (dated 1740).

1740   Meets Pope. Chaplain to the Prince of Wales. *A Seventh Letter, which finishes the Vindication of Mr. Pope's Essay on Man.*

1741   Meets Ralph Allen. *Divine Legation*, vol. 2.

1742   *The New Dunciad*, with commentary by Warburton. *A Critical and Philosophical Commentary on Mr. Pope's Essay on Man.* "Supplement to the Translator's Preface" in Charles Jarvis's translation of *Don Quixote.*

1743   Revised *Dunciad*, containing Warburton's "Ricardus Aristarchus of the Hero of the Poem."

1744   Pope dies. Zachary Grey's edition of *Hudibras*, with notes by Warburton. Editions of *Essay on Man* and *Essay on Criticism*, with commentary by Warburton. *Remarks on Several Occasional Reflections*, part 1.

1745   *Remarks on Several Occasional Reflections*, part 2. *A Faithful Portrait of Popery. A Sermon Occasioned by the Present Unnatural Rebellion. The Nature of National Offenses Truly Stated* (sermons).

1746   25 April, marries Gertrude Tucker, Ralph Allen's eighteen-year-old niece. Preacher of Lincoln's Inn. *An Apologetical Dedication to the Reverend Dr. Henry Stebbing. A Sermon preach'd on the Thanksgiving appointed to be Observed the Ninth of October.*

1747   Preface to Catherine Cockburn's *Remarks upon the Principles and Reasonings of Dr. Rutherford's Essay on the Nature and Obligations of Virtue*. Preface to John Towne's *A Critical Inquiry into the Opinions and Practice of the Ancient Philosophers*. Edition of Shakespeare.

1748   "The Editor to the Reader" in vol. 4 of Samuel Richardson's *Clarissa*. *A Letter from an Author to a Member of Parliament concerning Literary Property*. Pope's *Four Ethic Epistles* (i.e., *Moral Essays*), the so-called deathbed edition, with Warburton's commentary.

1749   Mid-March, mother dies. Begins correspondence with Richard Hurd. Thomas Newton's edition of *Paradise Lost*, with notes by Warburton. *A Letter to the Editor of the Letters on the Spirit of Patriotism*.

1750   *Julian*.

1751   Edition of Pope.

1752   Thomas Newton's edition of *Paradise Regained*, with notes by Warburton.

1753   Prebendary of Gloucester. *The Principles of Natural and Revealed Religion* (sermons), vol. 1.

1754   Chaplain to King George II. Doctor of Divinity degree conferred by the Archbishop of Canterbury. *A View of Lord Bolingbroke's Philosophy, Letters First and Second. The Principles of Natural and Revealed Religion*, vol. 2.

1755   Prebendary of Durham. *A View of Lord Bolingbroke's Philosophy, Letter the Third. A View of Lord Bolingbroke's Philosophy, Letter the Fourth and Last. A Sermon Preached . . . at the Parish-Church of St. Andrew, Holborn*.

1756   Early May, son, Ralph, born. *Natural and Civil Events the Instruments of God's Moral Government* (sermon).

1757   Dean of Bristol. *Remarks on Mr. David Hume's Essay on the Natural History of Religion*.

1760   20 January, consecrated bishop of Gloucester. *A Sermon Preached . . . in the Abbey Church, Westminster, on Wednesday, January 30, 1760*.

1761   *A Rational Account of the Nature and End of the Sacrament of the Lord's Supper*.

1763   Takes part in the prosecution of John Wilkes in Parliament. *The Doctrine of Grace*.

1766   *A Sermon Preached before the Incorporated Society for the Propagation of the Gospel in Foreign Parts*.

1767 *Sermons and Discourses on Various Subjects and Occasions.*

1769 Ruffhead's *Life of Pope,* based on materials supplied by Warburton and in part rewritten by him.

1775 Early summer, son dies. Intense depression. Rarely capable of sustained attention. Abandons attempt to complete third volume of *Divine Legation.*

1779 Warburton dies, 7 June. Buried in Gloucester Cathedral.

Chapter One
The Man

Some Contradictions

In 1820, a lead article in *Blackwood's Magazine* began by declaring that the two giants of eighteenth-century English literature were Samuel Johnson and William Warburton. About sixty years later, when a preacher in the cathedral where Warburton is buried mentioned him as one who had "lived among the men of Gloucester," the congregation began to buzz. "Warburton, Warburton?" someone was heard to ask. "Who was Warburton?"[1]

No man is entirely responsible for the vicissitudes of his own reputation, and Warburton has probably suffered more than most of his contemporaries from disparagement by hostile Victorians. Yet both fame and obscurity seem, paradoxically, his due. His first published prose work—a promising if undisciplined study in historiography—concludes with a paragraph plagiarized from John Milton. Though he pontificates frequently on the nature of Latin, Greek, and Hebrew style, his own Latin is full of errors, his translations from Greek sometimes depend on versions in Latin or French, and his Hebrew is nonexistent. His great *Divine Legation of Moses*—an enormously impressive compendium of speculative anthropology, theological polemics, literary criticism, and historical sociology—has as its express purpose the refutation of a deist argument that no deist had ever advanced. Generous, devout, full of good humor, and, with friends, tolerant and deferential, he is in print among the most arrogant and brutal controversialists that eighteenth-century England produced.[2]

Family influences. These contradictions of character and intellect are difficult to account for because none of his early biographers bothered to record the reminiscences of the people who knew him as a child. All that has survived of his early years are one or two anecdotes and the facts that appear in the Chronology above—brief, tantalizing glimpses of the circumstances that helped to shape his character. Two events that must have been crucial are the death of

his father in 1706 and his separation from his mother when he was
sent to school in Rutlandshire. If the loss of his father was traumatic,
however, he always concealed the scars, for he alludes to him only
once in all of his surviving correspondence, which consists of about
one thousand letters written over a period of sixty years.[3] It may be
significant, though, that throughout his life he formed strong attachments to older men such as his cousin and namesake William Warburton and the philanthropist Ralph Allen, whose niece he married.
There is also evidence that he was unusually devoted to his mother.
In a letter to his friend Dr. Robert Taylor, he called her "my dearest,
my incomparable Mother, whom I do more than love, whom I
adore."[4] Written in 1746 only a month after his marriage, this may
express as much guilt as love, for he had stayed close to home for
most of his forty-seven years and had moved away at a time when he
must have known she did not have long to live. According to Hurd,
after her death he seldom spoke of her without tears.[5] Freudians may
want to see in these symptoms of a strong Oedipal attachment some
connection with a rumor current in the 1760s that he was impotent
and did not father his wife's child. What evidence is available, however, suggests that the rumor was started by a young man posturing
as a rake and eagerly spread by Warburton's political enemies. Probably he was a genuine husband if not a passionate one.[6]

More significant than conventional Freudian sexual conflicts may be
the nature of his upbringing and his role as the eldest male child.
Hurd reports that in Brant Broughton his mother and sisters, fearing
that his habit of reading most of the night would ruin his health,
used to linger over evening coffee with him to try to keep him from
his books (W, 1:10). Though this anecdote is from his adult years, it
suggests that his character might have been affected by the "mater-
nal, child-oriented, affectionate and permissive mode" of child rear-
ing that arose in the middle ranks of English society during the
second half of the seventeenth century. Those reared in the older,
stricter mode were expected, even as adults, to behave toward their
parents with a detached, submissive formality and, in Warburton's
circumstances, would have been ordered to bed.[7] It is clear, at any
rate, that his mother was no formidable matriarch. Reminiscing
about her in a letter to Taylor, he recalls nostalgically "that happiness . . . when you and I were conversing together, while she was
giving us our coffee" (W, 1:117).

The dominance of men in eighteenth-century life also makes it probable that Warburton was the center of his family's attention, and he may have been especially indulged by parents whose first child had lived only a few days.[8] The early death of his father meant that when he came of age he would have to support the family, an eventuality not likely to reduce his importance in the household. Thus the notorious assertiveness of his style may have been learned at home. As Conyers Middleton told Lord Hervey, Warburton wrote "wth ye spirit of one, who has been used to dictate to ye Provincial Clergy around him"—and, he might have added, to the women around him as well.[9]

His role in the family may also help to account for his inability to tolerate equals. His most enduring friendships were with men who were older and more influential than he, or with younger men who were submissive or less fortunate. Real or apparent rivals he regarded with a jealous loathing. Though he had himself criticized the style of a Latin epitaph that William Stukeley had drafted for his late wife, he grew furious when he found out that the objections of another friend had persuaded Stukeley to abandon Latin for English. Stukeley's Latin, he fumed, was "much better than any that stupid pedant ever could write. . . ."[10] When David Hartley, later to become famous as the author of *Observations on Man,* began to practice medicine and serve as schoolmaster in Newark, Warburton evidently perceived as a threat to his own status as resident intellectual the presence of this intelligent, well-read, and apparently sweet-tempered young man. His letters to Taylor from this period are filled with malicious gossip about Hartley and ill-concealed hostility. Years after Hartley had left Newark, Warburton reported to Taylor a rumor that he was dead, adding with cold satisfaction, "I perceive his Discourse of the Inoculation [*sic*] quite spoiled his Character here as a Writer."[11]

But this unattractive side of Warburton was not the one that impressed his friends. If in print and occasionally in a letter he blustered and bullied, in face-to-face encounters he was said to be "good-humored," "easy," "entertaining," "tractable," "modest," "polite," "attentive"—so different, in fact, from his public persona that some of those who first met him after reading his works were moved to record their astonishment at the contrast.[12] If his early home life created the jealous bully, it presumably created the generous friend as well.

Friends and enemies. One possible explanation of this paradox is that, owing to the nature and intensity of his family attachments, he learned to divide the world too sharply between friends and enemies. It has been theorized that every child develops "social schemas"—that is, habitual expectations about the roles that people will play in relation to each other and to himself—and that the schemas of the first-born or only child take a typical form:

> As the child begins to perceive people outside the family, he places his parents at one end of certain dimensions and outsiders at the other end. He develops additional schemas, among which may be the following: (1) people who love and accept one (parents) are also people one loves; (2) people in the same group as oneself are more alike in some way than people who are not members of this group (strangers differ more among themselves than do members of the same family); (3) people who are close together have opposite and complementary social roles, since the father, mother, and child have opposite, complementary roles in the family.[13]

Any tendency to form such schemas would probably have been strengthened in Warburton by the shock of being sent away to school, an especially painful experience for the child of indulgent parents.[14] If it is true that his first master at Oakham thought him "the dullest of dull scholars,"[15] he must have felt with special poignancy the difference between his loving family at home and those outsiders who insisted on judging him by the abstract standards of scholarly competence. It is those outsiders, perhaps—a public of potentially hostile strangers—that he fears when the tone of his published prose degenerates from the assertive to the sneeringly defensive.

Some such division of the world into friends and enemies can be seen in the fierce loyalty that made him hypersensitive to the least hint of disrespect toward any member of his family. He snubbed the novelist Samuel Richardson on the street for having given his wife an edition of *Clarissa* to which, he wrongly thought, a slur on Alexander Pope had been added, and he pilloried Dr. John Burton in a note to the *Dunciad* for having published a harmless joke about Ralph Allen.[16] He also valued such loyalty in others. When Robert Lowth complained that his father had been insulted and plagiarized in Warburton's *Julian,* the latter replied that Lowth had every reason to be angry: "Had I known [that he was your father], I should not only have forborn complaining, but have applauded your piety. The injurer of your father's memory . . . deserved no quarter from you."[17]

Warburton extended the same kind of loyalty to his friends, reenacting with them, as it were, the roles of son and elder brother that he had learned in the family. As I have already pointed out, his most enduring friendships were with older men such as Sir Robert Sutton, Francis Hare, and Ralph Allen, all of whom he lost no opportunity to defend; or with younger, less fortunate or submissive men such as Taylor, John Towne, Hurd, and William Mason, to whom he gave advice and encouragement, and whose interests he labored to serve. Hurd says that he abandoned the law for the priesthood because he wanted to become a scholar, but the decision may also reflect the tendency of first-born children to take jobs that offer parentlike responsibilities (*W*, 1:4).[18] After he achieved fame, he liked to seek out promising young writers and offer them patronage. Ralph Heathcote thought that behind this ostensible generosity lay a sinister scheme for enlisting toadies,[19] but he seems really to have enjoyed serving as mentor to the young and insecure.

In return for his loyalty, he made heavy demands of his own. Older men kept his allegiance by using their power, wealth, or influence to advance his interests. It was not simply that he was ambitious, though ambitious he surely was, at least for fame. According to William Stukeley, he once said that he would give his eyes to be a Milton.[20] Beyond this, he regarded tangible generosity as the visible sign of love and expected his older friends to be as active on his behalf as he was on behalf of his own protégés. Some of his literary quarrels probably arose from the failure of his parental surrogates to play their assigned roles. Lewis Theobald, for example, was ten years his senior, and when they began to correspond in 1729, he had achieved both eminence and notoriety as the author of *Shakespeare Restored* and as the hero of the *Dunciad*. To this older, more eminent friend, Warburton devoted himself for seven years. For his sake he published three anonymous attacks on Pope in the *Daily Journal*. He sent him commentary on Shakespeare and criticized the commentary that Theobald sent him. He planned and wrote much of the preface to Theobald's *Shakespeare* of 1733. He solicited subscriptions. He gave advice and encouragement. But except for flattery and a generous public acknowledgment of Warburton's help with the *Shakespeare*, Theobald gave nothing tangible in return. He ignored the three *Daily Journal* articles when they first appeared, failing even to buy a copy of the second. He did not offer to make Warburton coeditor. He did not acknowledge publicly Warburton's contribution to the preface. He failed to keep his promise to return copies of his own letters, the originals of which Warburton had sent back to him at his request.

He failed to publish many of Warburton's notes but kept them in his possession as if surreptitiously planning to use them in a future work. He took all the profits of the *Shakespeare* to himself. When, in the spring of 1736, Warburton angrily wrote to complain of this treatment and to demand the return of his notes, Theobald was hurt and surprised, and genuinely believed himself innocent of dishonorable conduct. But Warburton was equally sincere in feeling betrayed. Expecting parental succor, all he got was thanks.[21]

Of his younger friends Warburton expected, if not public support for the positions he took in print, at least silence about them. It was not that he refused to tolerate criticism. As Hurd points out, when he sensed no hostility in the critic, he was as open to persuasion as anyone else (*W*, 1:104). He admitted with good-natured chagrin that Thomas Balguy had exposed a fallacy in one of his syllogisms, and he caused to be printed a letter from Conyers Middleton that contained, in his view, the most searching criticism of the *Divine Legation* that had ever been written.[22] What he could not tolerate was criticism— or what he took to be criticism—that was made public behind his back. Disagreements were either to be kept within the family or to be published with his approval, and in such a way as to stress the intermural nature of the debate. The most curious instance of his notion of literary etiquette is his sending to John Wesley for correction the manuscript of his *Doctrine of Grace*, a work largely devoted to attacking Wesley's evangelical enthusiasm.[23] Though Wesley was not a friend, he was a fellow Christian and a fellow clergyman, and Warburton, who admired him in spite of their theological differences, evidently believed that he deserved the courtesy of a prepublication warning.

The same sense of fraternity made him intensely bitter when he thought that someone who owed him loyalty had failed to defend him against his enemies or had unexpectedly joined them by criticizing him in public. Hurd remarks that "his resentment at the established clergy for their long and fierce opposition to [*The Divine Legation*] was the greatest weakness I ever observed in him" (*W*, 1:81)—a resentment caused by the failure of brother clergymen to behave like brothers. This resentment was almost certainly a motive in his decision to defend Alexander Pope's *Essay on Man*. Because this was the most important decision in Warburton's life and raises crucial questions about his moral integrity, it requires extended discussion.

The Background of the Vindication of Pope

The decision and its consequences. Late in 1738 Warburton discovered in the *Bibliothèque Raisonée des Ouvrages des Savans de L'Europe* a review of two pamphlets by the Swiss logician and theologian Jean Pierre de Crousaz, both works alleging that Pope's *Essay on Man* espoused an anti-Christian fatalism. Warburton could not have reacted more impetuously if he had come under attack himself. Without waiting to see either of Crousaz's pamphlets and arguing solely on the basis of extracts from one of them in the review, he rushed to Pope's defense with a 500-word letter in the *General Evening Post* and, at about the same time, with a ten-page letter in *The History of the Works of the Learned*. Though this second letter, supplemented by others, would eventually swell into a book, it was obviously written as a self-contained whole: neither its brief, businesslike introduction nor its abrupt conclusion promised a sequel. But Warburton was moved to write a second letter for the January issue of the *Works of the Learned* after he had read one of Crousaz's pamphlets. Again there was no indication that the defense was to continue. Then on 2 February 1738/39, Pope wrote to express his gratitude and to confirm Warburton's orthodox interpretation of the poem. With this encouragement he published four additional letters and, at Pope's suggestion, in late 1739 collected six letters—the five already in print in the *Works of the Learned* and an unpublished sixth—as *A Vindication of Mr. Pope's Essay on Man*.[24] Though he could not have known it, his defense of the poet had made his fortune and changed the course of English literary history. Pope would introduce him to the wealthy postal entrepreneur and philanthropist Ralph Allen, whose niece he would marry and whose influence would help to make him bishop of Gloucester. Pope would also make him his official commentator and literary executor. For better or for worse, Warburton, not Henry St. John, Viscount Bolingbroke, would edit the first posthumous collection of Pope's works, and Warburton's surrogate Owen Ruffhead, not Pope's friend Joseph Spence, would write the poet's official biography.

Warburton's decision raises two questions: (1) had he, as was rumored, once attacked the poem? (2) what motives impelled him to rush to its defense?

Early attitude toward the poem. The allegation that Warburton had once condemned the *Essay on Man* as "rank atheism" is supported mostly by the kind of malicious gossip that dogs every controversial writer.[25] Only one piece of testimony needs to be taken seriously, that by his long-time friend William Stukeley:

[Warburton] wrote a treatise against Mr. Popes essay on man, to prove it to be atheism, spinosaism, deism, hobbism, fatalism, materialism, & what not. In that my sentiments fully coincided. On a sudden he alter'd his style, & wrote a comment to prove the sublimity of that work. This did his business effectually. It brought him acquainted with Pope. Pope brought him acquainted with L.d Chesterfield, Bathurst, Burlington, Mr. Sollicitor Murray, &c., & this last got him to be preacher to Lincolns inn. Mr. Pope introduc'd him too to Mr. Allen of Bath, with whom he is become so great that Allen has married his niece to him, & effectually made his fortune.[26]

Though the commonplace book in which this appears was not published until the nineteenth century, Stukeley may be the source of all such stories. For instance, Samuel Johnson's later account of Warburton's indebtedness to Pope is similar to Stukeley's, repeating the error that the poet had introduced him to William Murray, whom Warburton had known at least since the spring of 1738.[27] Stukeley may also be the "late Dr. ———" who, according to Edmond Malone, said that "Warburton used to produce and read weekly essays in refutation of Pope's *Essay on Man*."[28] At any rate, of the people who allege that Warburton had initially condemned the poem, Stukeley is the only one who was personally acquainted with him in the 1730s and could have had firsthand knowledge of this attitude. Is Stukeley to be trusted?

Not entirely. This is not to say that Stukeley deliberately lied in his own commonplace book, only that allowance must be made for tricks of memory (he is obviously writing more than ten years after the event), for envy and resentment (he thought that fame had turned Warburton's head), and for a touch of dottiness.[29] Confidence is not inspired by his allegation that "Warburton got his legation notion from Saftsburys [*sic*] characteristics. . . ." What can this mean? If it means that Shaftesbury taught Warburton that Moses was divinely inspired in failing to teach the doctrine of a future state, it is obviously false. If it means only that Shaftesbury first called Warburton's attention to the absence of the doctrine in the Mosaic dispensation, it is plausible, but Stukeley says elsewhere that Warburton got the idea from Jean Le Clerc.[30] The truth is that in the privacy of his commonplace book Stukeley is able to vent his spleen without observing the niceties of accurate reporting. His testimony may not be wholly false, but it would be a mistake to put too much faith in it.

Moreover, even if Stukeley is right about Warburton's initial hostility toward the *Essay on Man,* he is wrong in suggesting that the defense was a sudden *volte-face.* As early as 1736 Warburton paid Pope the compliment of using the language of the poem to define the purpose of the *Divine Legation.* In early 1738, in the first edition of that work, he called Pope "A great modern Poet, and best judge of [epic writers'] merit," and, as Nadine Ollman points out, he designed part of his criticism of the *Aeneid* "to debate at a distance and in a most polite way with Pope." In the *Vindication of the Author of the Divine Legation of Moses,* published in April 1738, he praised Pope as "one of the politest men of the age."[31] The reversal of opinion, if such it was, began at least two years before the defense was written.

Motives. But why the defense? It is easy to imagine motives, some admirable, some not. It is probably significant that Warburton first alluded favorably to the *Essay on Man* at about the time of the break with Theobald. Seldom able to judge an idea apart from his opinion of the person who espoused it, he must have seen in a new light the works of his new enemy's enemy. There is also a suggestion in the letter to the *General Evening Post* and in the first two letters to *The History of the Works of the Learned* that his nationalism had been aroused by a foreigner's attacks on the greatest of living English poets.[32] His own account of his motives, however, deserves to be taken seriously. He said that he wanted to show the deists that Pope was not of their party, and that he especially resented the attacks on the poem because he too had been a victim of bigotry.[33]

Saving Pope from the deists was important to Warburton because he shared the concern of many other Christians of the period that infidelity had become intellectually fashionable. If the statistics of publication are any guide, the deists must have been outnumbered by at least fifty to one, but their ironic sneers at the faithful implied an exasperating complacency, as if their only opponents were a few feeble-minded bigots.[34] "It is come, I know not how," complained Joseph Butler, "to be taken for granted, by many persons, that Christianity is not so much as a subject of inquiry; but that it is now, at length, discovered to be fictitious. And accordingly they treat it, as if, in the present age, this were an agreed point among all people of discernment. . . ."[35] It is in the light of this competition for intellectual respectability that some responses to the *Essay on Man* must be judged. Norman Sykes points out that John Locke's name commanded such authority that both the orthodox and their opponents claimed him as an ally.[36] Pope's name had a similar cachet. This is not to say that disagreements about Locke's *The Reasonableness of Christianity* or the *Essay on Man* were merely cynical; it is to say, though, that people are naturally predisposed to find their most cherished beliefs confirmed or at least unchallenged by acknowledged genius. Writing to Pope for reassurance about the orthodoxy of the *Essay on Man,* Henry Brooke said that he had "often heard it insinuated, that you had too much wit to be that trifling thing called a Christian. . . ." At the same time, Pope and the *Essay on Man* were praised in the *Weekly Miscellany,* the most theologically conservative journal of the age.[37]

Warburton also feared that "infidelity [had] become so reputable as to be esteemed a test of superior parts and discernment," and in 1736 he had initiated a friendship with Conyers Middleton because, he later explained, he wanted to insure that so gifted a writer served Christianity rather than deism (*W,* 11:2, 5). The explanation rings true. He had nothing to gain from the friendship and much to lose. Middleton was strongly suspected of infidelity, and a theological controversy with Daniel Waterland had nearly cost him his librarianship at Cambridge and all of his degrees. Warburton's mentor Bishop Francis Hare expressed surprise that the friendship had been struck up after the controversy, when presumably Middleton had become a pariah.[38] Indeed, for praising him in the *Divine Legation,* Warburton was accused of infidelity by association, and his reply to the charge clarifies the reasoning that helped to inspire the vindication of Pope:

The opinion I have of [Middleton's] abilities, and of the sincerity of his professions, were the true reasons of that esteem I express for him; being desirous of allaying all disgust, if any hath arisen in him, from the treatment of his less candid adversaries; and of engaging him to a further and more compleat vindication of our holy faith, at a time when the good dispositions of the meanest advocate for Revelation should not, I think, in prudence be discouraged: Nay, was I so unhappy to think of [Middleton] as [a secret infidel] . . . I should be so far from estranging him further from the faith by uncharitable anathemas, that I should do all I could to court and allure him to *Christianity, by thinking well of its professors.* Thus much, I conceive, *Christian charity* would require; and how far *Christian policy* would persuade, let the *learned* say, who know what ornament his pen would be to the Christian faith. . . . (*W*, 11:5)

Possibly Warburton's motives in defending Pope were complicated by self-interest as they could not have been when he befriended Middleton. But he could also truly declare that in vindicating Pope he was doing his Christian duty by showing the "Libertines," as he called them, "that so noble a Genius was not of their party."[39] After all, no pen in England was a greater ornament to the faith.

Warburton also had good reason to sympathize with Pope as a victim of bigotry. Crousaz, who knew no English, had denounced, as Pope's, ideas that existed only in the French translations on which he had based his commentary. Even where the translations were accurate, he had chosen to interpret the poem in the most damaging way, assuming, for instance, that because a fatalist might express himself as Pope did, Pope must be a fatalist.[40] Warburton might well have been angered by such treatment of anybody under any circumstances, but there were two reasons why he especially identified with Pope.

First, whatever his opinion of the poem when it had originally appeared, by 1736 he had come to believe that he and Pope were engaged in a similar enterprise. Douglas White has pointed out that the *Essay on Man* is one of many eighteenth-century works that seek to refute deism by accepting deist assumptions.[41] Another such work is the *Divine Legation,* which, the title of early editions declares, is based "on the Principles of a religious Deist," and which, like the *Essay on Man,* is a kind of theodicy, concerned as much with the nature of God's justice in general as with its particular manifestations in the Mosaic dispensation. That Warburton recognized an identity of purpose between his own work and the poem is indicated by his alluding to Pope's phrase "to vindicate the ways of God to man" in a statement of his intention when he first publicly outlined the argument of *The Divine Legation* in 1736. This allusion became a direct quotation when the first volume was published in January 1737/8, almost a year before he began to defend Pope's poem (*W*, 7:302; 1:197).

Another reason for his identification with Pope was that he had had to contend with a Crousaz of his own—Dr. William Webster, editor of the *Weekly Miscellany.* Between February and July 1738, Webster had directly attacked or scornfully alluded to the *Divine Legation* in eleven issues of his journal.[42] Warburton was more profoundly affected by this vendetta than has generally been recognized. In addition to his acknowledged replies, he defended himself in several pseudononymous letters to newspapers and masterminded from behind the scenes an abortive plan to publish a collection of replies to Webster written by himself, Robert Taylor, and Lynford Caryl.[43]

He was not being hypersensitive, for Webster's attacks were outrageous. Accusing Warburton of undermining Christianity by pretending to support it, he managed to find evidence of subversion everywhere. For example, to illustrate the fourth of six alleged similarities between Warburton and "the infidels"—casting "*oblique* Reflections upon Christian institutions"—he cited Warburton's mention of the ass used to carry equipment in the Eleusinian Mysteries. What had this to do with Christianity? Why, Christ's "*riding* into *Jerusalem* on an *Ass* has been Matter of much wanton sport to the Infidels, and his Religion has been ridicul'd for its *mysterious Doctrines* and *Rites*. . . ."[44]

However absurd, Webster could not be dismissed as a crank. He had the support and, in at least one passage, the direct assistance of Daniel Waterland, one of the most respected theologians of the age.[45] He also managed to give his fulminations an air of respectability by linking them with a principled effort by high-church divines to enforce orthodoxy among the clergy. This policy had been expressed most dramatically in the successful opposition of Bishop Edmund Gibson and Richard Venn, Webster's collaborator on the *Miscellany,* to the appointment of Thomas Rundle to the bishopric of Gloucester on the grounds that, in private conversation, he had expressed a heretical view of Abraham's sacrifice of Isaac. In his first letter on the *Divine Legation,* Webster alluded to the Rundle affair by declaring that clergymen who expressed unorthodox opinions "in *Conversation* or from the *Press*" must clear themselves of suspicion or be denied ecclesiastical advancement. A month later he published a letter of apology from Pope's friend Walter Harte, who had been accused by Venn of expressing heterodoxy in a sermon, and introduced it by contrasting Harte's "*uncommon Integrity*" with the deviousness of a writer—obviously Warburton—who concealed his true opinions.[46] If Webster was intellectually beneath contempt, politically he looked dangerous.

One can imagine Warburton's state of mind in December 1738. He had been accused not of innocent error but of deliberate subversion; the arguments of his work had been grotesquely misrepresented; his accuser was himself a clergyman, had had the aid and support of other clergymen, and had sought, evidently with some success, to turn the clergy in general against him in order to ruin his career in the church. But there was no public outcry against this campaign of vilification; the published protests of two friends excepted, there was only silence. Who will doubt that, when he saw the *Essay on Man* clumsily misinterpreted and denounced, he felt a genuine rush of sympathy and identification? "When a great Genius," he wrote in his second letter to the *Works of the Learned,*

. . . shall happen to be enviously attack'd and wrongly accused, it is natural to think, that a Sense of Gratitude, due from Readers so agreeably entertain'd, or a Sense of that Honour resulting to our Country from such a Writer, should raise a pretty general Indignation. But every Day's Experience shews us just the contrary. Some take a malignant Satisfaction in the Attack; others a foolish Pleasure in a literary Conflict; and the far greater Part look on with a selfish Indifference.[47]

That "every Day's Experience" was his own.

A Final Mystery

The circumstances surrounding Warburton's decision to defend the *Essay on Man* suggest that he had nothing to be ashamed of. If his motives were mixed, the mixture contained much that is admirable: courage, impetuous generosity, sympathy for the victim of injustice. But whoever turns from the surrounding circumstances to the *Vindication* itself may have second thoughts. Maynard Mack remarks that the work has always been too easily dismissed,[48] and it may be that the belief that Warburton had once attacked the poem helps to undermine the credibility of his argument. On the other hand, the extravagance of the argument and the shrillness of the tone have made it easy for readers to believe that he had once attacked the poem. Indeed, the readiness of critics to assume the worst—that he changed Pope's poems without the poet's authority, that he lied about his relations with Sir Thomas Hanmer, that he was disliked by all who knew him—this readiness is traceable to a serious weakness in his character as a writer. An honest man in the ordinary affairs of life, he is occasionally transformed by ink as by some mysterious toxin. At such moments he has only to moisten his quill to begin posturing, exaggerating, inventing. Worse still, he is sincere. He believes his own inventions. Perhaps the most extraordinary example of this self-deception is his concocting an etymology based on a nonexistent Latin word, the phantasmal nature of which could have been discovered by anyone with a Latin dictionary.[49] No ordinary charlatan would ever have left himself so vulnerable to exposure and ridicule.

The cause of this strange deformity may lie buried in his childhood. Until more evidence comes to light than is available now, it can only be acknowledged without being explained.

Chapter Two

The Theologian

Divine Legation, Book 9

The posthumously published, incomplete book 9 of the *Divine Legation* contains Warburton's version of the religious history of the world from the creation till the birth of Christ (*W*, 6:213–399).[1] It reveals much about his theological doctrines and methods, and will serve as a useful introduction to the major theological works.

The religious history of the world.   From apparent inconsistencies between Genesis 1:26–27 and 2:7, 21–22, Warburton concludes that Adam and Eve were created outside of Eden and remained there for an uncertain length of time. During this period they lived by natural religion only. This he defines as the knowledge "That Man, endowed with REASON and FREEDOM of WILL, is a Moral Agent, and accountable for his conduct to his Maker; who hath given him, for his rule of Life, a Law, discoverable by the one Faculty, and rendered practicable by the other.—That the faithful Observers of this Law God will reward, and wilful Transgressors of it he will punish; but that, on repentance and amendment, he will pardon, and be reconciled to, Offenders" (*W*, 6:248). But the reward that reason alone teaches man to expect is not that of immortality. It is either an earthly reward—the manifestation of an extraordinary providence—or an unspecified postmortem reward that falls far short of eternal bliss.

Having approved the conduct of Adam and Eve under the dispensation of natural religion, God placed them in Eden. Here for the first time they were subject to revealed religion, including not only the moral dictates by which they had lived previously, but also a positive law: the prohibition against eating the fruit of the fatal tree. This law was a condition of God's free gift of immortality, a reward so far in excess of anything that man could do to deserve it that any condition that God might have set would have been trivial by comparison.

As a result of the fall, Adam and Eve reverted to their original condition. They had forfeited immortality, but natural religion taught them to expect the limited rewards that a beneficent maker would bestow upon the virtuous. By means of a special providence, God continued to grant such limited rewards until polytheism had everywhere destroyed natural religion. Then He revealed Himself to the Jews, governing their affairs, and theirs alone, by means of a special providence. This He withdrew when they too fell into idolatry, and by the time that they had once again purified their worship, the day of the third and final revelation had dawned.

By sacrificing himself on the cross, Christ restored to man the free gift of immortality that had been forfeited in Eden. Something more than man's repentance was required, for while he has a natural right to forgiveness if he sincerely repents, he has no such right to immortality. Nor could natural religion reveal the means by which immortality might be regained. A miraculous and arbitrary departure from God's moral government was required—the incarnation and sacrificial death of His son.

The crucifixion redeemed the gift of immortality for each man upon one condition—that he have "Faith in the Redeemer." This does not mean that faith without works is sufficient for salvation. Works are a qualification of eligibility for the gift of which faith is the condition. The distinction between a qualification and a condition is explained in the following analogy:

Suppose a British Monarch should bestow, in *free gift,* a certain portion of his own *Domaines* upon such of his subjects who should perform a certain service, to which they were not obliged by the stated Laws of that society under which they lived; it is evident, that the performance of this *last engagement* ONLY would be the thing which entitled them to the *free gift:* although that which gave them claim to protection, as Subjects, in the enjoyment of THEIR OWN PROPERTY, acquired by observing the terms of the contract between Subjects and Sovereign, was the necessary qualification to their claim of the *free gift;* since it would be absurd to suppose that this gift was intended for Rebels and Traitors, or for any but good and faithful servants of the King and Community.

As a note to this passage makes clear, private property is analogous to the rewards earned by obedience to the dictates of natural religion. Only by earning these rewards, through works, does man become eligible for salvation by faith (*W,* 6:306–7 and n.).

Besides restoring immortality to man upon the condition of faith in the redeemer, God condescended to secure that faith through the instrumentality of the Holy Ghost, who gives divine assistance—grace—to sincere believers. The purpose of grace is "to support our *Faith* and to perfect our *Obedience,* by enlightening the *understanding* and by purifying the *will*" (*W,* 6:317–18). The earliest manifestations of grace were miraculous, as in the gift of tongues. But, as Warburton declared in *The Doctrine of Grace* and would doubtless have declared in book 9 had he been able to complete it, miraculous grace ceased after the first ages of the church.

Doctrine.   Warburton is often difficult to locate on the spectrum of eighteenth-century theological opinion because he is so compulsively syncretistic. A typical example: elsewhere in the *Divine Legation,* he argues that, though some philosophers base morality on a moral sense, others on the essential difference between good and evil, and still others on the will of God, each group errs in failing to realize that all three are right (*W,* 1:233–35). Though a similar, if less paradoxical, syncretism informs his religious history of the world, it clearly places him at the anti-Augustinian end of the spectrum. To elements of Anglican orthodoxy he violently yokes elements of Pelagianism, the heresy named for the fifth-century English lay-monk Pelagius, who rejected Augustine's doctrines of original sin, grace, and predestination. Thus Warburton's belief that Adam was created mortal parallels, if it does not derive from, Pelagius's, and though Adam's death, as in orthodox doctrine, is a punishment for the fall, it is seen by Warburton as a reversion to nature rather than as a corruption of it. If he does not adopt Pelagius's concept of original sin as merely a bad example for the rest of mankind, neither does he adopt Augustine's concept of a universal moral infection. For Warburton the fall had no spiritual effects apart from man's temporary loss of immortality, and "What *Physical* contagion [the descendants of Adam] contracted at their birth, either of body or mind, is of little use to inquire . . ." (*W,* 6:259). Adam and Eve were as capable of living by natural religion after the fall as they had been before it, and generations of their descendants continued in the same reasonable faith.

Warburton's concept of grace is also more Pelagian than Augustinian. He nowhere states explicitly that Christians can be saved without grace, but he leaves open the possibility by habitually speaking of it as an aid to salvation rather than as a *sine qua non.* Notice in the fol-

lowing passage from *The Doctrine of Grace* that while reason is depre-
ciated, it is inferior to grace only because it is gradual in its efficacy:

We know it to be morally impossible for Reason, however refined and
strengthened by true Philosophy, to root out, on the instant, the inveterate
habits of Vice. All that this magisterial Faculty can do is, by constantly repeating her dictates, and inforcing her conclusions, gradually to win over
the Will; till, by little and little, the mind accustoms itself to another set
of ideas, productive of other practices and other habits. A work of time and
labour! as those good men have sufficiently experienced, who, on a mere rational conviction, have attempted and perfected a change in their lives and
manners.

If Christians have, "on a mere rational conviction, perfected a change
in their lives and manners," then perhaps they have, "on a mere
rational conviction" that Christ is the redeemer, been saved. Non-
Christians—not infidels but those unavoidably ignorant of Christ—
are certainly saved without grace (*W*, 8:306; 6:315–16). Warburton
leaves no doubt as to their eligibility for salvation, while limiting
grace by definition to the faithful.

In the preface to *Julian,* Warburton declares in his typically forth-
right manner that Augustine's anti-Pelagianism is "the most absurd
opinion that ever was" (*W*, 8:xvi–xvii). It is a little surprising that
so fierce an opponent of infidelity should espouse so relatively "soft"
a doctrine of sin and salvation. Trained in the law, he may have
found appealing Pelagius's legalism, for as John Passmore remarks,
"Pelagius' approach is . . . a lawyer's: what kind of legislator would
he be who set up laws nobody could obey and then punished his subjects for not obeying them?"[2] Compare Warburton's analogy quoted
on page 16 above between God and an English monarch. But Warburton's God is even more permissive than the God of Pelagius, who,
because he believed in absolute free will, expected men to be eternally
damned if they abused it.[3] Warburton's God punishes disobedience
not, it seems, by inflicting pain, but only by withholding rewards.
"In Dr. Warburton's hypothesis concerning the efficacy of repentance, and God's character as a rewarder," a hostile critic of book 9
complains, "the mercy and goodness of God are continually brought
forward; but we hear nothing of his attribute of righteousness and

justice. . . ."[4] Though the phrase "future state of reward and punishment" runs like a litany through the rest of the *Divine Legation* and his other theological writings, Warburton never specifies the nature of the punishment, nor does he ever commit himself on the question of its duration.[5] It is as if he cannot bring himself to believe that God could be more severe than his own apparently permissive parents.

Assumptions. Book 9 also reveals two related and perhaps unconscious assumptions that appear repeatedly in Warburton's works: uniformitarianism and utilitarianism.

Uniformitarianism is Arthur O. Lovejoy's term for the belief that "reason . . . is identical in all men; and [that] the life of reason therefore . . . must admit of no diversity."[6] I use the term in preference to rationalism, which, insofar as it implies the opposite of empiricism, is misleading with respect to a good Lockean like Warburton. He does not doubt that all knowledge is derived from the senses, but usually assuming that men always and everywhere reason in the same way, he discovers in the past the intellectual fashions of the present. He is convinced, he writes Thomas Balguy, that "every people in the same situation & circumstances will always have the great outlines of every political[,] domestic & religious System the same."[7] In fact, he identifies eighteenth-century habits of thought even where the "situation and circumstances" are unique. Adam and Eve living alone outside of Eden before the fall construct, by a process of logical inference, the same minimal religion an eighteenth-century intellectual like Warburton would have constructed if he had not had the advantage of divine revelation. Revelation itself is an appeal to the modern critical intelligence, God's miracles having been performed not so much to awe men into faith as to provide evidence that reason can use to distinguish true revelation from false.

By utilitarianism, a corollary of Warburton's uniformitarianism, I mean the belief that self-interest rightly governs human conduct. Man is so constituted as naturally to seek happiness, a drive that God uses for His own ends. Earlier I mentioned Warburton's reconciling three conflicting views of the basis of morality. This he does by arguing that God exploits men's interests and aptitudes to incite them to moral conduct. Aesthetes respond to the moral sense, intellectuals to the rational distinction between good and evil, and ordinary men to the spur of an express command (*W,* 1:235). Ideally all three types will seek to maximize the pleasure they take in beauty, cerebration, or obedience. God reveals many other truths by means of utility:

> For, TRUTH AND GENERAL UTILITY NECESSARILY COINCIDE; that is, Truth is *productive* of Utility; and Utility is indicative of Truth. That truth is *productive* of utility, appears from the nature of the thing. The observing truth, is acting as things really are: he who acts as things really are, must gain his purposed end: all disappointment proceeding from acting as things *are not*: Just as in reasoning from true or false principles, the conclusion which follows must be necessarily right or wrong. But gaining this end is utility or happiness; disappointment of the end, hurt or misery. If then Truth *produce* utility, the other part of the proposition, that utility *indicates* truth, follows of necessity. For not to follow, supposes two different kinds of GENERAL UTILITY relative to the same creature, one proceeding from truth, the other from falsehood; which is impossible. . . . (*W,* 3:217–18)

Such reasoning leads him to conclude that, "till the infidels be convinced that religion is useful to society, they will never be brought to believe it true." And thus it leads him to base on frankly utilitarian grounds the arguments of two of his three major theological works.

The Alliance between Church and State

In defense of the status quo. *The Alliance between Church and State,* Warburton's first important book, was originally conceived as part of the *Divine Legation* but was published separately in 1736, two years before the more sensational work went to press. His theory of church-state relations, he declares, "was formed solely on the contemplation of nature, and the unvariable reason of things." Imagine his astonishment, therefore, when it turned out to mirror in every detail "the church and state of England" (*W,* 7:166). It is this kind of flourish that so often weakens his credibility. The truth, of course, is that from beginning to end the *Alliance* is a defense of the status quo. On the other hand, the reasoning of the book is deductive and does draw conclusions from the "unvariable reason of things." In contrast to Jonathan Swift, for instance, who thought that nations might differ so radically in climate, soil, history, and cultural genius that no single ecclesiastical system would serve for all of them,[8] Warburton assumes a uniformitarian ideal of church-state relations to which every nation should, and to which England does, conform.

The status quo that he pretends not to have started with is the somewhat disorderly, ad hoc arrangement that had evolved since 1688 from the push and shove of Whig–Tory conflict: to wit, an established church whose clergy were maintained by the state through the collection of tithes and whose bishops were selected by the crown and sat in the House of Lords; and—inconsistently, it seemed to many—a limited toleration, that is, on the one hand, the legal existence of dissenting Protestant trinitarian churches, and on the other, a Test Act that in theory, though seldom in fact, barred the members of such churches from holding civil or military office by requiring as a condition of eligibility the annual taking of Communion according to the rites of the Church of England. To high-flying Tories, the inconsistency lay in toleration; to radical Whigs, in establishment. Warburton's task was to make rational the compromise that offended both extremes.

The argument.   Religion and civil government, Warburton reasons, are both essential to society, the former because it compensates for unavoidable deficiencies in the latter, such as the inability to restrain private vices. But religion itself must be a society owing to the nature of man, who, unlike the angels, is incapable of the bodiless worship of God. He requires articles of faith and a ritual. The purity of these requires a common policy and officers authorized to enforce it. This constitutes a society. But this society is concerned exclusively with the soul and is thus independent of civil society, which is concerned only with the body. Society as a whole is best served when these two independent societies unite out of mutual self-interest. The church is protected by the state, and the state benefits from promotion by the church of public and private morality, on which the health of any nation depends.

How does the state protect the church? One way is by insuring that the clergy are properly provided for—through the collection of tithes, for instance. Another is by granting certain of the clergy seats in the legislature. Another is by establishing a test law, "some sufficient proof or evidence required from those admitted into the administration of public affairs, that they are members of the religion established by law" (*W*, 7:242). A test protects the church by keeping its enemies out of positions of authority which they might

use to destroy it. But there is no contradiction between a test law and
the *"divine doctrine of toleration"* (*W,* 7:274). On the contrary, the test
law makes toleration possible by insuring that diversity of religion
will not be a danger to the state.

Success of the work. No defense of establishment was likely
to win the approval of radical Whigs, who attacked the *Alliance* as
soon as it was published.[9] Its appeal to a wide range of opinion
within the church, however, is suggested by the praise it received
from the conservative William Webster and the liberal Francis Blackburne, both of whom would later become Warburton's enemies.[10]
One source of this appeal was probably the tone of the book. The
Alliance is among the least rancorous of Warburton's works, though
truculent notes were added to later editions. "As to the Form," he
wrote in the preface to the first edition, "the subject being of the
greatest weight and gravity in itself, and here treated abstractedly, I
have aimed at nothing, in the style, but exactness in the expression,
and clearness in the construction . . . ." (*W,* 7:iii). This aim he largely
achieved, and, in doing so, eschewed the satire that often enlivens
but sometimes disfigures his other works.

Another reason for its appeal may have been his ingeniously adapt-
ing to church-state relations the contract theory of government. This
theory was anathema to conservatives,[11] but even they must have been
pleased to see it turned against radical Whigs in support of the established church. To those who might wonder where the contract between church and state was to be found, Warburton wittily replied
that it was stored "in the same *archive* with the famous ORIGINAL
COMPACT between magistrate and people, so much insisted on, in
vindication of the common rights of subjects" (*W,* 7:165).

A further reason for the broad appeal of the *Alliance* was Warburton's utilitarian argument that an established church and a test law
are rational and just irrespective of the truth of the religions involved.
Since the business of the magistrate is not with the soul, the state
allies itself impartially with the church of the majority, whatever it
may be—episcopal in England, presbyterian in Scotland. This argument led to charges that Warburton had resurrected Thomas
Hobbes,[12] but it minimized disagreement by excluding from the debate the emotionally charged issue of which church in England best
embodied the will of Christ, and by supporting the broadest possible
comprehension, since "the larger the religious society is, where there

is an equality in other points, the better enabled it will be to answer the ends of an *alliance* . . ." (*W*, 7:242–43). The work thus stood a chance of getting a fair hearing from at least moderate dissenters. It probably also got a hearing from skeptics who would have disdained a purely theological argument but who shared the widespread belief that a national religion was needed to reconcile the majority to the inevitable inequities of a hierarchical society.

The *Alliance* also countered, indirectly but unmistakably, the most divisive Christian polemicist of the age, Bishop Benjamin Hoadly. In his notoriously controversial Bangorian sermon of 1717, Hoadly had made the individual's conscience the only authority in matters of the spirit, thus destroying the church's very reason for being. The *Alliance* replied that while every man has a God-given right to his own religious opinions, any church composed of human beings requires a social organization. And any social organization, if it is not to be destroyed from within, must have the power to expel those who refuse to abide by its rules. Even the Quaker William Penn, Warburton shrewdly observed, was forced against his principles to create an establishment with a test law. *The Alliance between Church and State* thus tried to reconcile—and for many readers did reconcile—the tenets of Whig individualism with existing ecclesiastical authority. [13]

The Divine Legation of Moses

Deism. *The Divine Legation of Moses* is Warburton's contribution to the deist controversy which had been raging in England since the end of the seventeeth century and would burn itself out by the middle of the eighteenth. The term "deist" was as carelessly applied as terms like "communist" or "fascist" in our own day, and genuine deists might disagree as much among themselves as with their orthodox opponents about the content of their faith. Essentially, however, deism is the belief that nature is the only source of knowledge about God and His attributes. It thus poses two crucial issues. Is supernatural revelation possible? If it is possible, has it actually occurred? [14] *The Divine Legation* replies in effect to the second question, advancing the thesis that Jews in the Mosaic dispensation experienced the continuous miracle of God's active intervention in their daily affairs.

The argument. Accepting the challenge of a test by deistical "reason," Warburton argues that the silence of the Pentateuch about the existence of an afterlife of rewards and punishments proves, contrary to deist doctrine, that ancient Judaism was divinely inspired. This paradox is developed in the following syllogisms:

I. Whatsoever religion and society have no future state for their support, must be supported by an extraordinary providence.
The Jewish religion and society had no future state for their support.
Therefore the Jewish religion and society were supported by an extraordinary providence.

II. It was universally believed by the Ancients, on their common principles of legislation and wisdom, that whatsoever religion and society have no future state for their support must be supported by an extraordinary providence.
Moses, skilled in all that legislation and wisdom, instituted that *Jewish* religion and society without a future state for its support.
Therefore *Moses* who taught, believed likewise, that *this* religion and society were to be supported by an extraordinary providence. (*W,* 1:201)

Volume 1, consisting of books 1 through 3, supports the major premise of each syllogism, book 1 being devoted to the first, books 2 and 3 to the second. Volume 2, consisting of books 4 through 6, supports the minor premise of each syllogism. Book 4 supports the premises *per se,* book 5 defines the nature of the Jewish state, and book 6 considers all passages from the Bible that had been thought to prove the existence of the doctrine of a future state among the ancient Jews. The unfinished volume 3 was to consist of books 7 through 9. Book 7 was to trace the religious doctrines of the Jews from the earliest prophets to the Maccabees, book 8 was to vindicate Moses,[15] and book 9 was to explain his silence about the doctrine of a future state and to give "a general view of the whole course of God's universal economy from Adam to Christ." Parts of book 9 were published posthumously and have been summarized at the beginning of this chapter.

This bare outline cannot begin to suggest the convolutions of the argument or the wealth of knowledge brought to bear in its development. Book 2 will serve as an example (*W,* 1:297–348; 2:1–210). The defense of the proposition that "The ancient Lawgivers universally believed that such a Religion could be supported only by an extraordinary Providence" is divided into two parts, the first concerning what we would call political science, the second concerning philosophy. Every ancient lawgiver, Warburton argues, instituted and supported a state religion, and every religion, the Jewish excepted, was founded on the doctrine of an afterlife of rewards and punishments. (The latter proposition he deduces as follows in book 1: since religious faith is undermined by the inequality of rewards and punishments on earth, it can be strengthened and maintained only by a belief in postmortem justice.) Quoting liberally from Plutarch, Cicero, Seneca, Sextus Empiricus, Heroditus, and Lucian to prove the universality of religion in the ancient world, he reasons that it must have been established and supported by the state. For one thing, the absence of religion in primitive societies such as that of the Indians of Canada proves that it cannot survive unless it has been institutionalized. For another, the fact of state support can be inferred from the nature of pagan religion. It is said to have consisted in the worship of deified mortals, in a view of the gods' attributes parallel to the character of the government (benign gods derive from benign governments, tyrannical from tyrannical), and in public worship more concerned with the well-being of society than with the morality of the individual.

How did ancient political leaders go about establishing religion? First, they claimed divine inspiration, as is evident from the practice of magistrates in Egypt, Greece, Rome, China, Peru, Scandinavia, and the Mogul Empire. Since such claims would have been unnecessary merely to secure respect for the laws, it follows that they were made in order to establish religion. Second, ancient magistrates taught the doctrine of a providence. Here Warburton goes out of his way to cross swords with Richard Bentley, citing the prefaces to the laws of Zaleucus and Charondas, and, in a digression of eighteen pages, challenging Bentley's argument in the *Dissertation on the Epistles of Phalaris* that these were spurious. Finally, Warburton declares that ancient legislators supported the doctrine of a providence by instituting mystery religions, which were devices for inculcating a belief in a future state of rewards and punishments. This last proposition leads to a seventy-eight-page discussion of the nature and function of the Eleusinian Mysteries and to interpretations of the *Aeneid,* book 6, and *The Golden Ass* of Apuleius, the one illustrating the social utility of the Mysteries, the other illustrating the religious. Book 2 concludes by reemphasizing the political importance of a belief in the afterlife, a belief that, Warburton declares, is essential to religion and so natural to the mind of man that it can survive even the loss of the religion to which it was originally attached.

Weaknesses of the *Divine Legation.* The paradoxical thesis
of the *Divine Legation* is inherently implausible and suggests the doctrine preached by Peter Devries's fictional clergyman the Reverend
Andrew "Holy" Mackerel—that God's omnipotence is proved by His
ability to save us despite His nonexistence.[16] And Warburton probably invented the argument against which the thesis is directed, or, if
he did not invent it, groundlessly attributed it to the deists. This is
a serious charge, but the evidence for it seems overwhelming. First,
Warburton nowhere documents the alleged deist denial of the divine
origin of the Pentateuch on the grounds that it lacks the doctrine of
a future state.[17] Second, later scholarship has failed to discover such
a denial by any deist before the *Divine Legation* was written.[18] Third,
almost twenty years after the publication of the work, Bolingbroke
advanced the deist argument in question, declaring that he had never
seen it before. Warburton and John Leland record this boast but do
not challenge it, though both are at pains to expose Bolingbroke's
lack of originality (*W*, 5:222–23).[19] Fourth, in reply to Bolingbroke,
Warburton asserts that the deists "agreed so far with *Atheism,* as to
confine the whole of man's existence to the present life" and that "the
final purpose of [orthodox arguments] against Deism is to prove a FU-
TURE STATE" (*W*, 1:293). But the argument of the *Divine Legation*
requires that the deists believe in a future state and disparage the
Pentateuch because the doctrine is not taught therein. Fifth, in reply
to Henry Stebbing's *An Examination of Mr. Warburton's Second Proposition* (1744), Warburton attributes not to the deists but to conservative Christians the view that, without the doctrine of a future state,
the religion of the Pentateuch would be unworthy of God (*W*,
11:307). Warburton may be trying to allay his own doubts by pro-
jecting them onto his deist enemies, but whatever his motives, the
thesis of the *Divine Legation* combats a phantom.[29]

The book is also weakened by its uniformitarian assumptions. The
debate between Christians and deists was as much about the nature
of man as about the nature of God, and Warburton's natural man is
a deistical rationalist. This is true, as I have shown, of his Adam and
Eve, and it is equally true of their pagan progeny. They turned to
religion not because they were awed by the mystery of the universe
or had spiritual needs that they were driven to satisfy, but because
they were calculating utilitarians who recognized the political benefits
of religious institutions. This is a variation on the belief of certain
deists that all religions except their own were created by the self-in-

terested cunning of priests. Also like many deists, Warburton ignores the power of tradition and custom. Even if religion had originated as he supposes, it would not follow that later generations of political leaders continued to weigh its utility as if it were nothing more than, say, a traffic law. That religion might be interconnected in subtle and obscure ways with all the other institutions of society and that political leaders themselves might be caught in the network—such possibilities the *Divine Legation* does not consider.

A more serious weakness is the assumption that the doctrine of postmortem judgments is essential to the survival of civilized societies. Though belief in some kind of afterlife is nearly universal, belief in rewards and punishments is not. In some cultures life after death has been imagined as painful for good and bad alike; in others it has been thought to'perpetuate the inequities of earthly life, the rich enjoying beyond the grave the privileges of their earlier status.[21] The major premise of Warburton's first syllogism is not supported by the facts.

Nor is this error the result of insufficient anthropological evidence. Many of Warburton's contemporaries, including those who doubted the existence of an afterlife, believed that the doctrine was crucial to social stability, for without the hope of future recompense or fear of future retribution, all but the best of men would be incapable of practicing the social virtues.[22] Many also shared Warburton's belief that general utility is a sign of truth. The relation between this belief and the supposed utility of the doctrine of an afterlife is lucidly stated by John Leland:

Now the great usefulness and necessity of this doctrine is no small argument of its truth. For if men are so framed, that they cannot be properly governed without the hopes or fears of a future state; if these are necessary to preserve order and good government in the world, to allure and engage men to virtue, and deter them from vice and wickedness; this shews that the Author of their beings designed them for immortality, and a future state, and that consequently such a state there really is; except it be said, that he formed our nature so as to make it necessary to govern us by a lie, and by false motives, and imaginary hopes and fears.[23]

The major premise of the first syllogism rests, in fact, on a foundation of conventional wisdom that determines Warburton's reading of what anthropological evidence was available to him.

This reading of the evidence in the light of the premises is evident in a number of ways. For example, book 2 is intended to prove that belief in the utility of the doctrine of an afterlife was universal. But since the doctrine is assumed to be inseparable from religion (that of the ancient Jews excepted), every quoted reference to the utility of religion is taken as evidence of a belief in the utility of the doctrine of a future state (*W, 2:298–99*). A similar misinterpretation of the evidence appears in the discussion of the Eleusinian Mysteries, the secret ceremonies of an ancient cult associated with the goddesses Demeter and Persephone. Warburton's claim to have discovered that the purpose of these was to inculcate a belief in a future life cannot be dismissed out of hand, but there are no grounds for supposing that the doctrine involved a universal judgment of the dead. Though initiates might have looked forward to blissful immortality, nothing suggests that noninitiates were thought to be rewarded or punished according to their deserts, and the requirement that initiates not be guilty of murder—evidently the sole moral condition of initiation—was probably intended only to keep the ceremonies unpolluted.[24] The evidence for a limited conception of a future state is so interpreted as to imply a belief in a broader, and essentially different, doctrine.

Another weakness of the work is structural. Many readers have praised Warburton's skill in architectonics, and it is true that the *Divine Legation* is remarkably lucid considering the wealth of material it encompasses. Warburton was clever at discovering relations between remote topics, a gift that led Lewis Theobald to ask him to write the transitions in Theobald's preface to his edition of Shakespeare.[25] But ingenuity of transition cannot disguise disproportion. A house whose pantry is larger than its ballroom is poorly designed no matter how attractive the corridor between them. Many sections of the *Divine Legation*—on the Mysteries, on the *Aeneid,* on Egyptian hieroglyphics—are much longer than their contribution to the argument would warrant, and opposing arguments often seem arbitrarily selected for refutation. The disagreement with Richard Bentley in book 2, for instance, is unnecessary by Warburton's own admission, since "were it as [Bentley] supposes, the fragments [of Zaleucus and Charondas] would be rather stronger to our purpose" (*W, 1:324*). Laurence Sterne was not exaggerating when he compared the *Divine Legation* with Swift's *A Tale of a Tub* and his own *Tristram Shandy*.[26]

Merits of the *Divine Legation*.   For all its deficiencies of content and form, the *Divine Legation* has a kind of clumsy grandeur. Its very magnitude, the volume and variety of learning it assembles and disposes, would be impressive even if its every argument were fallacious and every interpretation false. It is a virtual encyclopedia of seventeenth- and eighteenth-century ideas about antiquity—its history, philosophies, mythologies, modes of worship, literature, and systems of writing. In his too-great eagerness to debate, Warburton went out of his way to include as targets for attack countless quotations and summaries of opposing views. If the *Divine Legation* survived a general holocaust in which every book published in England between 1650 and 1750 were destroyed, it might be possible to re-create from its pages a reasonably accurate picture of what that century knew and believed about the ancient world.

The book also has virtues apart from its value as a document. Though Warburton was not the first to discover the silence of the Pentateuch about a future state—the point had been made by the Anabaptists in the sixteenth century, and Warburton himself cites Bishop George Bull, Hugo Grotius, and Simon Episcopius[27]—he was the first to examine the question with scholarly thoroughness. This took courage, since most contemporary Christians held the view that the doctrine was at least implied in the Pentateuch, and the seventh of the Thirty-nine Articles of the Church of England declares that "both in the Old and New Testament, everlasting Life is offered to Mankind by Christ," and that "they are not to be heard, which feign that the Old Fathers did look only for transitory Promises." As late as 1863 Mark Pattison accused Warburton of extremism, asserting that while the doctrine is not stated in the Pentateuch, it was probably taken for granted. In 1879 a theologian more sympathetic to Warburton complained that in spite of the *Divine Legation* the "far-reaching consequences" of the question were still being ignored.[28] In the twentieth century, however, Warburton's position is the conventional wisdom of both Christian and Jewish scholars.[29] And however paradoxical his interpretation of the fact, Warburton correctly recognized that interpretation must be problematical for Christians. Confronting the question of why God permitted the ancient Jews to remain ignorant of postmortem rewards and punishments, a twentieth-century Catholic theologian is forced to conclude, "We cannot pretend to fathom the depths of the wisdom of God. . . ."[30]

The *Divine Legation* also has the virtues of its defects. Some sections whose disproportionate length disfigures the whole have intrinsic value as essays independent of the unconvincing thesis they are supposed to prove. A case in point is the discussion of Egyptian hieroglyphics, which was translated into French and independently published in two volumes in Paris in 1744. The ostensible purpose of this section is to help prove the great antiquity of Egyptian culture, the nature of which, according to Warburton, must be clarified if the purpose of Moses' policies is to be understood. But what is important in the section is a brilliant guess, based on inspired common sense, about the origin and evolution of Egyptian writing. Scornfully rejecting the Neoplatonic mysticism of Anasthasius Kircher, the seventeenth-century German Jesuit who had interpreted each hieroglyph as a symbol of an esoteric metaphysical concept, Warburton begins from the assumption that writing is invented to satisfy practical, workaday needs. Civilized people have to keep records, and sometimes they have to communicate over long distances. Sound being evanescent, writing is invented to serve these two purposes, and an obvious way to begin is to draw pictures of the things to be represented. Such an approach to the problem of Egyptian writing is judged by a modern scholar to be "unprejudiced, intelligent and critical," and while Warburton repeats some traditional errors of detail, he comes "almost deceptively close to the truth."[31] He shrewdly infers, for example, that hieratic, a cursive form used for copying religious and literary works, developed out of hieroglyphics as a "running-hand." Pictures, he reasons, were difficult and time-consuming to draw, so they were gradually transformed into simplified characters that nevertheless retained some of the marks of their imagistic origin. He thus correctly explains the process by which Egyptian writing evolved from pictographs to a system of arbitrary signs. This theory had no immediate practical results, but indirectly it may have contributed to the later successes in decipherment of Thomas Young and Jean Francois Champollion. By convincingly routing the older view of hieroglyphics as the repository of arcane knowledge, it helped to make them an object of genuine scientific study.[32] It was praised and quoted in France by Étienne Bonnot de Condillac, Charles de Brosses, and Anne-Claude-Pellipe de Caylus, and was given the imprimatur of avante-garde orthodoxy when it was incorporated word for word into the *Encyclopédie*.[33]

Theological influence of the *Divine Legation*.   Other merits of the *Divine Legation* will be discussed in chapter 3. It remains to ask whether the work served the theological purpose for which it was written. Certainty is impossible when scholars fail to agree even about the outcome of the deist controversy as a whole, one seeing the triumph of orthodoxy, another the defeat of both orthodoxy and deism at the hands of skepticism.[34] But allowing for the ambiguities of the evidence, it seems probable that the *Divine Legation* made few converts and might have driven some readers into the arms of infidelity. The American Revolutionary War general Charles Lee said that, intending to become a Christian, he had read the *Divine Legation* and come away hating the Old Testament God.[35] Lee may be too eccentric to serve as a witness, but, reviewing the history of the deist controversy in the middle of the century, John Leland implied his opinion of the work by devoting to it less than a single sentence[36]— this despite the fact that it was probably the most widely read attack on deism to appear in the twenty years before Leland published.

The provocative nature of the work may have undermined its effectiveness as a defense of orthodoxy by calling into question beliefs that had generally been taken for granted. What must have been its effect on ordinary readers who had always assumed that the doctrine of a future state was taught in the Pentateuch? Many might have been convinced by Warburton's masterly demonstration of its absence, but few could have had their faith confirmed by the paradox he wanted its absence to prove. The influence of the work seems to have been most extensive among freethinkers and skeptics who plundered its encyclopedic riches but scorned its Christian message. Warburton's treatment of pagan myth, one scholar has observed, "broached new questions which were more and more divorced from theological concerns. . . ." Voltaire is known to have borrowed heavily from the *Divine Legation* in his *Philosophie de l'histoire,* especially in the chapter on the Eleusinian Mysteries, and no less than twenty-three articles in the *Encyclopédie* are based on (most, indeed, plagiarized from) the *Divine Legation* and *The Alliance between Church and State.*[37] The result of Warburton's defense of the faith was probably to strengthen the enemy.

Julian

The argument. If the *Divine Legation* argues for God's continuous intervention in the lives of early Old Testament Jews, *Julian* defends the authenticity of a single miracle. In 363 the Roman emperor Julian encouraged the Jews in Jerusalem to rebuild their Temple, which had been destroyed by Vespasian and Titus in the first century. The project was abandoned when an apparent earthquake destroyed the still unfinished building and killed a number of workmen. Christian historians saw the hand of God in this disaster, reporting such phenomena as a whirlwind; thunder and lightning; falling fire that melted tools; an invisible impediment in the doorway of a nearby church that prevented Jews from seeking safety inside; a cross within a circle glowing in the sky; and almost indelible glowing crosses impressed on the clothes and bodies of eyewitnesses. Warburton undertakes to prove that the reports are true and the events miraculous.

A miracle was required, he argues, because "The truth of Christianity must stand or fall with the ruin or restoration of the Temple at Jerusalem. . . ." God had so constituted Judaism that its essence could be destroyed upon the establishment of Christianity. Since sacrifices were fundamental to this merely preparatory religion, and since they could be performed only at the Temple in Jerusalem, the destruction of the Temple was the virtual destruction of the faith—a destruction darkly prophesied in both testaments. When Julian set out to restore the Temple, he believed that he could demonstrate the fraudulence of Christianity by giving the lie to its prophecies. Indeed, God Himself "seems to have raised up this extraordinary man on set purpose to do the 1st honours to the Religion of *Jesus;* to shew the world what human power, with all its advantages united, was able to oppose to its establishment" (W, 8:34–49).

Having shown that the occasion was important enough to deserve a miracle, Warburton argues that a miracle occurred. He proves that the partly restored Temple was actually destroyed, for this is reported by pagan and Jewish sources as well as by Christian. The pagan historian Ammianus Marcellinus, a friend of Julian's, even mentions the eruption of balls of fire near the foundations. Moreover, "had the fact [of the destruction] been *groundless,* its falsehood must have been known to thousands: and what was so easy to be disproved, the interests of thousands would have exposed" (W, 8:67–94).

The bulk of Warburton's argument is devoted to answering objections, the most challenging of which concern the credibility of the uncanny details reported by the Church Fathers and other Christian historians. Can Gregory Naziansen be believed when he speaks of a mysterious force that kept the Jews from finding safety in a church; of a whirlwind and earthquake; of a cross within a circle in the heavens; of glowing crosses burned into clothes and flesh? Yes, Warburton replies, because all of these seemingly supernatural events have a natural explanation. The panic-stricken Jews trying to force their way into the church believed themselves miraculously opposed when actually they were immobilized by the crush of the crowd. A whirlwind naturally accompanies an earthquake. The cross within a circle "was neither more nor less than one of those meteoric lights, in a still and clouded sky, which are not infrequently seen in solar or lunar halos." The crosses on the clothes and bodies of the witnesses were produced by lightning, which is known to strike in extraordinary ways and to leave regular figures. The crosses glowed because they were phosphorescent (*W*, 8:114–41).

Of the various other objections that Warburton answers, one follows from his own explanation. Has he not proved that the earthquake and its effects were wholly natural? It is true, he concedes, that the earthquake has all the marks of a natural disaster, but then if it did not, nobody would credit the story at all. Besides, there is evidence that the initial cause was miraculous. The Temple was so situated that a fiery eruption was unlikely; the effects of the quake were confined to the immediate area; and the fire burned only so long as the workmen persisted in approaching the building, subsiding when they were driven back by the flames (*W*, 8:202–13).

To the objection that religious conflicts are so common that any natural disaster can be made to seem an expression of divine displeasure, Warburton offers a more general answer. If the miracle involves a messenger from God and the suspension or reversal of the laws of nature, the messenger has only to declare its purpose. But a miracle like the destruction of the Temple, "performed by the *immediate power* of God, without the intervention of his servants, in which only a *new direction* is given to the Laws of Nature," is proved genuine only if it has been prophesied or if it is "seen to interpose so seasonably and critically as to cover the honour of God's moral Government from insult." The destruction of the Temple, unlike the supposed pagan miracle of the annihilation of Brennus's forces at Delphi, meets both conditions (*W*, 8:213–25).

One other argument is worthy of notice, an argument based on the theory of probability. What are the chances, Warburton asks, that an earthquake would occur just when the Temple was being restored, and in an area where earthquakes are rare? What are the chances, however natural the cause, that a fire would rise and fall with the approach and withdrawal of the workmen, and that a cross would appear in the sky, and that crosses would appear on the bodies and clothes of witnesses? What are the chances that an earthquake in the area would have occurred on only one other occasion, that of the Crucifixion? And what are the chances that no attempt would ever again be made to restore the Temple? "To compute the immensity of these odds," Warburton concludes, "will exceed all the powers of Numbers" (*W*, 8:225–26).

Weaknesses of *Julian*. *Julian* is an unfinished book. When Warburton started the presses running in 1749, almost a year before it was published, the argument was to consist of three parts: "The first, to establish the truth by human testimony, and the nature of the fact. 2. An Answer to Objections. 3. An Enquiry into the *nature* of that evidence which is sufficient to claim a rational assent to the miraculous fact."[38] But, after announcing these topics on the title page, in the text he conflates the first two and declares that the third "will afford a subject for another discourse" (*W*, 8:34).[39] Readers who bought the book on the promise of the title page could have used the services of a Consumer Protection Agency.

Apart from false labeling, the omission of the third topic weakens the theoretical foundations of the book. John Henry Newman, who admired the work and drew on it heavily in his *Two Essays on Biblical and Ecclesiastical Miracles,* complained of a passage on miracles in the *Divine Legation* that Warburton "begins by saying that miracles which subserve a certain object deserve our attention, he ends by saying that those which do not subserve it do not deserve our consideration, and he makes himself the judge whether they subserve it or not."[40] The same fallacy governs his reasoning in *Julian.* To be sure, a fullfledged argument would not necessarily have improved his logic, but it might have led him to realize that finding a universally acceptable criterion for judging miracles is formidably difficult. The truth of the matter aside, his too-easy solution to the problem is rhetorically ineffective, suggesting a superficiality that reflects unfavorably on other aspects of the book.

To a reader familiar with his earlier works, the paradoxes in his argument begin to look mechanical. Contradictions between pagan and Christian accounts of the event, he declares, "are so far from invalidating the fact, that they add to its support." In recounting fantastic details such as glowing crosses and the like, "the Fathers could have said nothing more corroborative of our account." On the other hand, a miracle must seem natural or nobody will believe it—it is confirmed, in other words, by the credibility of the very scientific explanations that rule it out (*W,* 8:106, 120, 210). Exhilarating if specious in the *Divine Legation,* such paradoxes have become a formula or an involuntary reflex.

Merits of *Julian.* As history, nevertheless, *Julian* is an impressive book. It combines a shrewd, thorough, and scholarly examination of sources with an elegance and purity of style that are seldom evident in Warburton's other works. Both virtues can be seen in the following passage on the reliability of Ammianus Marcellinus as a historian:

> He was a pagan, and so not prejudiced in favour of Christianity: He was a dependent, a follower, and a profound admirer of *Julian,* and so not inclined to report any thing to his dishonour: He was a lover of truth, and so would not relate what he knew, or but suspected, to be false: He had great sense, improved by the study of philosophy and knowledge of the world, and so would not easily suffer himself to be deceived: He was not only contemporary to the fact; but, at the time it happened, resident near the place: He recorded the event not on its first report, when, in the relation of journalary occurrences, much falsehood blends itself with truth; but after time and enquiry, which separates the impure mixture, had confirmed what was real in the case: He related it not as an uncertain report or hearsay, with diffidence; but as a notorious fact, at that time, no more questioned in *Asia,* than the project and success of the *Persian* expedition: He inserted it not for any partial purpose; in support or confutation of any system; in defense or discredit of any character: He delivered it in no cursory or transient memoir; but gravely and deliberately, as the natural and necessary part of a composition the most useful and important, a general History of the Empire; on the complete performance of which the author was so intent, that he exchanged a court life, for one of study and contemplation; and chose *Rome,* the great repository of these materials, for the place of his retirement. (*W,* 8:69)

From conflicting accounts of the destruction of the Temple in Christian, pagan, and Jewish sources, Warburton carefully derives a chronology of events, beginning with a storm and concluding with the appearance of a glowing cross in the sky (*W,* 8:135–39). Much of this is based on scientific theories that reflect his wide reading in the contemporary literature of earthquakes and lightning. The inadequacy of these theories, to be sure, undermines the plausibility of his account, but his method of proceeding is one that any well trained twentieth-century historian would use in attempting to explain the phenomena on other than supernatural grounds. Moreover, *Julian* avoids the error, unfortunately prominent in the *Divine Lega-*

tion, of assuming that ancient beliefs straining the credulity of modern intellectuals must be the product of calculated deception. He suggests, for instance, that medieval Christian historians jumbled the chronology of events surrounding the destruction of the Temple because, certain that each event had a separate miraculous cause, they would have regarded an attempt to find a natural order in the phenomena as not only hopeless but sacrilegious (*W*, 8:135). This observation may well be true and reflects a sophisticated historical sense, an awareness that the reliability of ancient sources must often be judged in the light of alien habits of thought.

Some conclusions. Besides sermons, Warburton published four theological works in addition to those discussed above: *Remarks on Several Occasional Reflections* (1744–45), a collection, in two parts, of replies to various critics of the *Divine Legation; A View of Lord Bolingbroke's Philosophy* (1754–55), an attack in four letters on Bolingbroke's posthumously published deistical works; *Remarks on Mr. David Hume's Essay on the Natural History of Religion* (1757), assembled by Hurd from Warburton's notes on Hume's book; and *The Doctrine of Grace* (1762), in part a defense of the orthodox view of inspiration in the New Testament, and in part an attack on the claims to inspiration by John Wesley. Mostly defensive, none of these deserves to rank with the major works, though *The Doctrine of Grace* contains an important essay on relativism in literary taste that might have transformed his criticism if it had come earlier in his career.

His Pelagianism aside, Warburton's theology often looks more radical than it is. He likes to adopt an unorthodox position—that the establishment of a religion does not depend on its truth, that the Pentateuch contains no reference to postmortem rewards and punishments, that the destruction of the Temple in Jerusalem can be scientifically explained—and then to turn the position to the advantage of orthodoxy. This procedure gives rise to his notorious paradoxes. Whether it is a desperate attempt to be original at all costs, or whether it serves to make thinkable, ideas he might otherwise have found too threatening to contemplate, it is the source of what is worst and what is best in his theology.

Chapter Three
The Critic

Pope called Warburton "the greatest general critic I ever knew."[1] In current histories of eighteenth-century criticism, however, Warburton is scarcely mentioned, and in anthologies he does not appear at all. This discrepancy between Pope's extravagant praise and twentieth-century neglect seems to imply an error in judgment somewhere, but it may result in part from the ambiguity of the word "criticism," which in literary histories usually means "literary theory." If distinctions are made between Warburton's theoretical, historical, and interpretive criticism, perhaps his current obscurity can be reconciled with the good judgment of both Pope and twentieth-century literary historians.

Theoretical Criticism

Rejection of critical extremes. Like many other eighteenth-century Englishmen, Warburton distrusts system-builders and says so frequently. So it is not surprising that he fails to devise a system of his own. In his preface to his edition of Shakespeare he rejects two critical extremes in favor of "NATURE and COMMON-SENSE." At one extreme, he thinks, is "such a sort of criticism as may be raised mechanically on the Rules which Dacier, Rapin, and Bossu have collected from Antiquity; and of which such kind of Writers as *Rymer, Gildon, Dennis and Oldmixon,* have only gathered and chewed the husks. . . ." At the other extreme is "the plan of those crude and superficial Judgments, on books and things, with which a certain celebrated Paper so much abounds; too good indeed to be named with the Writers last mentioned, but being unluckily mistaken for a *Model,* because it was an *Original,* it hath given rise to a deluge of the worst sort of critical Jargon. . . ."[2] He rejects, in other words, both French rationalism and its English imitations, and Joseph Addison's essays on "the Pleasures of the Imagination," the only criticism in the *Spectator* that can be said to have popularized a new jargon.

Critical rationalism. Despite his stated preference for Addison, Warburton's theoretical criticism is closer to French rationalism than to the psychologism of "The Pleasures of the Imagination." Temperamentally he was drawn to rationalism in two ways. An almost Puritanical feeling of guilt about neglecting theology for criticism is probably responsible for his excessive emphasis on the didactic function of literature at the expense of imaginative intensity. In a long defensive passage in the preface to Shakespeare, he imagines "some *Tartuffe* ready, on the first appearance of this edition, to call out again, and tell me, that *I suffer my self to be wholly diverted from my purpose by these matters less suitable to my clerical Profession.*" He replies to this imaginary charge in a variety of ways, primarily by stressing the "knowledge of our Nature" that Shakespeare teaches, "a lesson which can never be too often repeated, or too constantly inculcated . . ." (*S,* 1:xxiv). Especially revealing of his emphasis on didacticism is a note in the edition of Pope that may reflect on Addison's glorification of descriptive poetry in *Spectator* no. 416. "The use of a pictoresque [*sic*] imagination," Warburton writes, "is to brighten and adorn good sense; so that to employ it only in description is like childrens delighting in a prism for the sake of its gaudy colours. . . ." In another formulation, description lacks even the frivolous merit of "gaudy colours" and must itself be vivified by morality: "Descriptive poetry is the lowest work of Genius. Therefore, . . . Mr. Pope . . . never fails . . . to enoble it with some moral stroke or other."[3]

Warburton's "rationative virtuosity," as it has been called, also impels him in the direction of rationalism. He assumes that good poems are methodically planned because, one suspects, he is clever at discovering a method even where none exists. He accepts the conventional eighteenth-century contrast between Shakespeare the natural genius and Ben Jonson the laborious craftsman, but with a significant, though not an original, qualification: *The Tempest* and *The Merry Wives of Windsor* show that Shakespeare knew "the rules of art" and that in his other plays he deliberately pandered to a philistine audience. "The Truth is," he writes elsewhere, "no one thought clearer, or argued more closely than this immortal Bard." He finds in Pope's *Essay on Man* "a precision, force, and closeness of connection rarely to be met with, even in the most formal treatises of Philosophy," and he rejects Addison's belief (*Spectator* no. 235) that in the *Essay on Criticism* "the observations follow one another like those in Horace's *Art of Poetry,* without that methodical regularity which would have been requisite in a prose writer." Pope's poem, he replies, is "a regular piece," and he wonders "how *method* can hurt any one grace of Poetry; or what prerogative there is in verse to dispense with regularity" (*P,* 4:152n.; *S,* 1:xv–xvi; *P,* 3:150n., 1:138n.).

Related to this emphasis on rationality is his ridicule of Edward Young's *Conjectures on Original Composition.* Young, he tells Hurd, "is the finest writer of nonsense, of any of this age" because he fails to understand that the source of originality lies "in the manner, and not in the matter."[4] Warburton has been accused of defining originality so as to insure the supremacy of Pope,[5] but he is primarily concerned to minimize the difference between poetic and other genius. As will become apparent below, he believes that all thought worthy of the name is primarily rational, so that the philosopher or the scientist differs from the poet only in manner of expression.

It is evident from his remarks on Shakespeare that he believes in "the rules of art." Ben Jonson, he thinks, was forced by lack of genius to cultivate the rules and so contributed to the advancement of English drama. He ridicules the complaint of Thomas Rymer that because soldiers are conventionally bluff and guileless, Iago's deviousness is unnatural. But instead of rejecting all such rules of characterization, he invents a new one of his own: Individual representatives of a class or profession may be characterized in any way the author pleases as long as a majority of such representatives in the play are properly stereotyped. On the other hand, he nowhere applies the rules to an entire play, and he deplores their mechanical application to new works, which, because "*Nature* is exhaustless," may create rules of their own (*P,* 4:152–53n.; 1:150n.; *S,* 8:404, n. 8). If he accepts a conventional rule in theory, he is not necessarily satisfied with conventional justifications for it. With mixed results, he tries to base the dramatic unities on firmer ground than the old argument from credibility that Samuel Johnson would later demolish:

the artful and yet natural introduction of the persons of the Drama into the scene, just in the nick of time . . . is the supreme beauty of Comedy, considered as an *action.* And as it depends solely on a strict observance of the *Unities,* it shews that the *Unities* are in nature, and in the reason of things, and not in a mere arbitrary invention of the *Greeks,* as some of our own country *critics,* of a low mechanick genius, have, by their works, persuaded our *wits* to believe. For common sense requiring that the subject of *one comedy* should be *one action,* and that the action should be contained nearly within the period of time which the representation of it takes up; hence we have the unities of *Time* and *Action;* and, from these, unavoidably arises the third, which is that of *Place.* For when the whole of one *action* is included within a proportionable small space of *time,* there is no room to change the *scene,* but all must be done upon one *spot of ground.* Now, from this last unity (the necessary issue of the two other, which derive immediately from nature) proceeds all that beauty of the *catastrophe,* or the winding up of the plot, in the ancient comedy. For all the persons of the Drama being to appear and act on one limited spot, and being by their interests to embarrass, and at length to conduct the action to its destin'd period, there is need of consummate skill to *bring them on,* and *take them off, naturally* and *necessarily:* for the grace of action requires the one, and the perfection of it the other. Which conduct of the action must needs produce a beauty that will give a judicious mind the highest pleasure. On the other hand, when a comic writer has a whole country to range in nothing is easier than to *find* the persons of the Drama, just *where* he would have them; and this requiring no art, the beauty we speak of is not to be found. (*S,* 6:23–24, n. 2)

The appeal to "common sense," especially in support of the unity of time, shows that Warburton is still under the spell of pseudo-Aristotelian tradition, and it is not clear why he thinks that it is harder to bring characters together in a single setting than in many. But he is surely right to emphasize the pleasure of watching an artistic difficulty gracefully overcome, a pleasure lost whenever formal constraints are abandoned for the different but not necessarily superior advantages of freedom. It should also be noticed that he does not claim too much. He defends the unities in comedy only—presumably the unities in tragedy would have to be justified on other grounds—and limits the "supreme beauty" of the unities to the play "considered as an action." Considered in other ways, successful comedy would display other beauties.

Addisonian criticism. Where Warburton's theoretical criticism is indebted to Addison, it is usually tinged by a heavier emphasis on the rational and the didactic than is present in "The Pleasures of the Imagination." The purest parallel to the latter occurs in a note to Shakespeare. As Addison in *Spectator* no. 419 praises Shakespeare's "noble extravagance of fancy" in that "fairy way of writing" which "quite loses sight of nature," so Warburton extols *The Tempest* and *A Midsummer Night's Dream* as "the noblest Efforts of that sublime and amazing Imagination, peculiar to *Shakespear,* who soars above the Bounds of Nature, without forsaking Sense; or, more properly, carries Nature along with him beyond her established Limits."

Even here the qualifying phrase "without forsaking Sense" tempers the Addisonian enthusiasm. Another parallel involves the psychology of the poet, who according to Addison must "be able to receive lively ideas from outside objects, to retain them long, and to range them together, upon occasion, in such figures and representations as are most likely to hit the fancy of the reader." In a note on Pope, Warburton echoes this passage but deemphasizes affective immediacy in favor of regularity of organization: "the Art of Poetry consists in *selecting,* out of all those images which present themselves to the fancy, such of them as are truly poetical. . . . in the Poet this faculty [that is, that which causes judicious selection] is eminently joined with a *bright imagination,* and *extensive comprehension,* which provides stores for the selection, and can form that selection, by proportional parts, into a regular whole. . . ."[6]

The clearest example of Warburton's conservative aesthetic is contained in a long section of Owen Ruffhead's *Life of Pope,* the section replying to Joseph Warton's depreciation of the poet in his *Essay on the Genius and Writings of Pope.* The use of Ruffhead needs a word of explanation. It is known that Warburton supplied the biographical information for Ruffhead's book; that Ruffhead adopted some of this material verbatim; that he used, also verbatim, much of the commentary from Warburton's edition of Pope; that Warburton corrected the proof sheets, making substantial changes that appear in the published version; and that he made more corrections in the reply to Warton than in any other section of the book. It therefore seems reasonable to conclude that Ruffhead here speaks for Warburton, thus providing a longer passage of theoretical criticism than the latter ever wrote on his own.[7]

The Ruffhead–Warburton defense of Pope asserts rather than reasons, repeats itself, and digresses at length on minor issues. My concern, however, is not with the quality of the argument but with its theoretical implications. The following propositions, the foundation of the defense of Pope, summarize Warburton's literary theory insofar as this can be inferred from his meager and scattered remarks on the subject.

(1) *The primary function of poetry is to teach.* Echoing in language and thought a sentence from the preface to Shakespeare, Warburton–Ruffhead declare, "The end of literary compositions of every kind, should be to enlarge the understanding and mend the heart." Notice the absence of any reference to pleasure. This contrasts not only with

the literary hedonism of Warburton's friend and disciple Richard Hurd, but with such moderate variations on the Horatian teach-delight formula as that by Samuel Johnson: "The end of poetry is to instruct by pleasing" (*S,* 1:xxiv).[8]

(2) *The greatest poetry teaches by appealing to reason.* Curiously, the argument in support of this view is indebted to "The Pleasures of the Imagination," though Addison is made to yield a conservative conclusion. Borrowing from Francis Bacon, Addison in *Spectator* no. 418 extols the imagination because it can satisfy that longing in man for "something more perfect in matter than what it finds there. . . ." Warburton–Ruffhead complain that this very tendency of the imagination betrays even "the greatest writers" into "bombast" or "ridiculous whining":

> The reason is, that in these kinds of poetry, nature is generally represented in the *outre.* The imagination loves to be flattered; it always pictures to itself something more grand and more extraordinary, than it ever met with in reality: and there is always something in every scene, which falls short of the perfection it aspires to. This propensity is favourable to poetical enthusiasm, and is what gives such a peculiar relish to the sublime and pathetic. But to be extravagant, requires less skill than is usually imagined; and to describe nature in her genuine character, is perhaps the greatest effort of art.

Warburton–Ruffhead also use Addison's distinction between the pleasures of sense, imagination, and understanding. Reading the original and derivative versions side by side will show the extent of the borrowing and, more important, the changes in emphasis by which Warburton–Ruffhead make right reason the supreme poetic value.

Addison

The pleasures of the imagination, taken in their full extent, are not so gross as those of the understanding. The last are, indeed, more preferable, because they are founded on some knowledge or improvement in the mind of man; yet it must be confessed that those of the imagination are as great and as transporting

Warburton–Ruffhead

The pleasures of the imagination are more obvious, but they certainly are not so refined, as those of the understanding. The latter are attended with some increase of knowledge, on which the mind may, from time to time expatiate by reflection. The former, though transporting for a time, are confined

Addison   Warburton–Ruffhead

as the other. A beautiful prospect
delights the soul as much as a demonstration, and a description in Homer hath charmed more readers
than a chapter in Aristotle. Besides,
the pleasures of the imagination
have this advantage above those of
the understanding. It is but opening the eye, and the scene enters.
The colors paint themselves on the
fancy, with very little attention of
thought or application of mind in
the beholder. We are struck, we
know not how, with the symmetry
of anything we see, and immediately assent to the beauty of an object without inquiring into the
particular causes and occasions of it.

in their effects and are quickly evanescent. The pleasures of the imagination seem to hold a middle space
between the gross enjoyments of
sense, and the more refined delights
of the understanding. All are, in
some degree, capable of enjoying
the two former; but very few have a
relish for the latter: as very few are
capable of such a stretch and per-
severance of thought, as alone can
render them grateful.

It is owing to the indulgence of
this excessive license of flattering
the imagination, that, at an advanced age, as judgment ripens, the
greater part of poetry becomes in-
sipid. . . . the species of poetical
composition which is most excellent
. . . is certainly that, for which our
relish does not abate with the
growth of our experience and
understanding.[9]

(3) *Great poetry subordinates imagination to a moral or intellectual purpose.* This proposition follows from number 2 and parallels Warburton's depreciation of descriptive poetry quoted on page 38 above.
Conceding that "poetry may be allowed, more than any other literary
composition, to be addressed to the imagination," Warburton–Ruffhead insist that "without being directed to any purpose, either moral
or intellectual, it certainly does not deserve to be ranked among the
most excellent species of poetry."[10]

(4) *The essence of poetry is style.* This follows from the belief that reason is common to all modes of thought: "As to the faculty of mind,
to which [poetry] properly refers, that depends altogether on the nature of the various objects it treats of, and which are common to
prose as well as verse." The poet may think philosophically, for example, and the philosopher imaginatively: "No man will venture to
deny, that *Longinus* and *Quintilian, Locke* and *Newton,* &c. though no
poets, were all men of imagination." Since all thought is essentially
the same, differing only according to the requirements of different

subject matters, it follows that style alone distinguishes the poet from other writers.[11]

Theory versus taste. Nothing I have said about Warburton's rationalism should be construed to mean that he had narrow, old-fashioned tastes in literature or that he was insensitive to imaginative intensity. On the contrary, he read and admired works by contemporary writers as various as Richardson, Fielding, Gray, Sterne, Byrom, Churchill, Rousseau, Voltaire, and Macpherson.[12] It is possible that his theory is rooted in his attachment to Pope. Nadine Ollman argues that his criticism changed in the direction of conservatism under Pope's influence, but of this I am not so sure. Since he had few occasions to write theoretical criticism before he met Pope, what seems change may be only the first appearance in print of long-held views. On the other hand, Ollman correctly points out that he sounds more conservative when writing about Pope than when writing about other poets. His theory is colored by the poetic mode he happens to be discussing.[13]

Two similar notes on different poets will illustrate the difficulty of justly characterizing a piecemeal theorist who made no effort to be consistent. The first is a note that he contributed to Thomas Newton's edition of *Paradise Regained*. "Popular or philosophical opinions," he declares, "have their use indifferently in poetry. And which soever it be that affords the most beautiful image, whether that founded in the truth of things, or in the deceptions of sense, that is always to be preferred."[14] Possibly this can be reconciled with the denigration of descriptive poetry cited earlier in this chapter if "beautiful image" is taken to mean "beautiful image used in the service of moral truth." But consider this note on Pope: "It is sufficient that a principle of philosophy has been generally received, whether it be true or false, to justify a poet's use of it to set off his *wit*. But to recommend his *argument* he should be cautious how he uses any but the true. For falsehood, when it is set too near, will tarnish the truth he would recommend" (*P,* 1:143). While there is just enough difference between "beautiful image" and "wit" to leave open the possibility that Warburton distinguished between images used in description and those used in argument, there is still a *prima facie* inconsistency between declaring, on the one hand, that "which soever affords the most beautiful image . . . is *always* to be preferred" (my italics) and, on the other, that "falsehood . . . will tarnish the truth." Moreover, the inconsistency, if such it is, reveals no movement toward conservatism. The note on Milton appears after the note on Pope.

Warburton wrote almost no theoretical criticism apart from defending or annotating specific poets. Since the poet to whom he devoted most of his attention inspired his most rationalistic criticism, the emphasis in his theory as it is preserved in print is heavily conservative. But the other, Addisonian, strain in his thought, exemplified by the note on Milton, never entirely disappeared. If circumstances had linked him with a mid-century poet as closely as they linked him with Pope—with William Collins, say, or one of the Wartons—he might have expressed more fully an outlook that evidently stayed with him to the end of his life but that seldom found its way into print.

Historical Criticism

It is a commonplace of eighteenth-century criticism—indeed, the idea can be traced back to the Renaissance—that when judging a poem the critic must consider the conditions in which it was written.[15] These calls for the study of historical contexts often coexist, as they do in Warburton, with the application of wholly ahistorical literary standards, or lead to nothing more concrete that Warburton's observation cited above that Shakespeare broke the rules to please the ignorant. To my knowledge, however, Warburton is the only critic of the period to suggest that an ineradicable ignorance of the past makes it impossible for a modern audience to respond fully to an ancient poem. In a note on Pope, he declares that an advantage of modern works is that "our intimate acquaintance with the *occasion of writing,* and the *manners described,* lets us into all those living and striking graces which may well be compared to that perfection of imitation only given by the colouring: While the ravage of Time amongst the monuments of former ages, hath left us but the gross substance of ancient wit, so much of the form and matter of body as only may be expressed in brass or marble" (*P,* 1:191 n.). Even if true, this generalization can never be proved, since the only evidence that might support it is the recovery of "those living and striking graces" whose loss the generalization requires. The possibility of its truth, however, can inspire a salutary caution in the critic of ancient literature. Warburton makes this point in a practical way in a note on

Shakespeare. He writes that a dead metaphor (one "grown so common as to desert, as it were, the figurative") can be properly mixed with another metaphor because the former "is not apt to excite in us the representative image" and "the mind is already gone off from the image to the substance." He then warns critics who might be tempted to correct mixed metaphors in Greek or Roman works that "the much-used hacknied metaphors being now very imperfectly known, great care is required not to act in this case temerariously" (*S,* 2:266–67). That Warburton seldom practices the caution he urges on others does not diminish the value of the doctrine.

Besides these brief remarks on the relation between literature and historical conditions, Warburton wrote three essays in literary history. None has merit as a factual account of the literary past, but all are interesting as pioneering efforts in tracing the evolution of genres.

The history of chivalric romance.   The first appeared in 1742 as a supplement to Charles Jervis's preface to his translation of *Don Quixote* and was later reprinted in two parts, the first—on chivalric romance—as a note to *Love's Labours Lost,* and the second—on drama—as a note to *Richard III.*[16] Chivalric romance, according to Warburton, originated in Spain and is based on the pseudo-Turpin and Geoffrey of Monmouth. The heroes and settings are usually Spanish, and the subject matter is the wars of Christians against Saracens. The element of the marvelous originated not in Spain but in the East, whence fantastic tales were brought by returning Crusaders and pilgrims. These tales were believed by the travelers themselves, by the people in general, and by the writers who incorporated the marvels into their romances. When the Spanish borrowed from Geoffrey of Monmouth, they changed Saxons into Saracens, either by mistake, or more likely, by design, because chivalry was so closely associated with the wars against the Moors.

This account Warburton patches together from the description of Don Quixote's library in chapter 6 of Cervantes's novel, from a little knowledge of Spanish history, and possibly from a reading of Claudius Salmasius and Sir William Temple.[17] Nowhere does he give evidence of knowing firsthand the works whose titles he so authoritatively (and in two instances erroneously) cites.[18] The entire essay is itself a kind of romance, a parody of historical scholarship that would not be out of place in the antiworld of Vladimir Nabokov's *Ada,* where events have taken a different turn from those on earth. But no novelist would be guilty of Warburton's vagueness.

This vagueness, almost certainly the result of deliberate obfusca-
tion, has seemed to acquit Warburton of at least two charges leveled
by his severest critic. In 1780, Thomas Tyrwhitt "trounced"—the
word is René Wellek's—Warburton's essay so thoroughly as to have
immortalized, in the opinion of Edmond Malone, the "futile performance" that had provoked it.[19] Tyrwhitt points out that the heroes
and settings of the old romances are not normally Spanish, that only
a few such works are concerned with the wars against the Saracens,
and that, *pace* Warburton, one of these is not *Amadis de Gaul*. Trying
to make sense of Warburton's ambiguities, however, Tyrwhitt makes
an error of his own. On the evidence of *Don Quixote*, Warburton declares that *Amadis de Gaul* was the first of the older romances to be
printed, neglecting to say when it was written. Tyrwhitt supposes
that it must have been written shortly before it was printed. Since
later scholarship has discovered references to the work from the middle of the fourteenth century, Warburton's silence about its date of
composition creates an illusion of prescience, as if he had anticipated
the discoveries of the twentieth century. Actually there is no evidence
that he had guessed an early date of composition or that he was even
interested in the chronology on which any reliable history must be
based.

Tyrwhitt appears to commit another blunder when, in reply to
Warburton, he declares that there are no Saracens in Geoffrey of
Monmouth. Warburton does not say that there are. He says that the
Spanish changed Geoffrey's Saxons into Saracens. Tyrwhitt, however,
is calling attention to equivocation in the following passage:

> the subject of those Romances were the *Crusades* of the *European* Christians
> against the *Saracens* of *Asia* and *Africa*.
>   Indeed, the wars of the Christians against the Pagans were the general
> subject of the Romances of *Chivalry*. They all seem to have had their
> ground-work in the two fabulous monkish Historians: The one, who, under
> the name of *Turpin* Archbishop of Rheims, wrote the History and Atchieve-
> ments of Charlemagne and his twelve Peers; . . . the other, our Geoffrey of
> Monmouth.

Tyrwhitt notices the shift from "*Crusades* . . . against the *Saracens*"
to "wars . . . against the Pagans" and points out that the change is
necessary because "our Geoffrey has nothing like a crusade, nor a single Saracen in his whole history. . . ."[20] He might have added that

Warburton's word "ground-work" is meaningless because he never specifies the content of Spanish borrowings.

The history of mystery and morality plays. The brief history of pre-Shakespearean drama is superior to the essay on romance because, assuming that mystery and morality plays are lost, Warburton does not have to pretend to have read them or to squirt clouds of ink to conceal his ignorance. He tries to reconstruct the contents of the plays from secondary sources, and though his conclusions are usually wrong, they are at least reasonable given the paucity of evidence available to him. Unfortunately, his dogmatic tone is inappropriate to his speculative and erroneous conclusions.

He knows that mystery plays arose in Western Europe after the dark ages, that they were "a representation of some scripture-story," and that they included comic elements. He makes no connection between the form of the plays and Catholic liturgy, however, and he is unaware that miracle plays dramatized the lives of saints. Assuming the identity of the French *moralité* and the English morality play, and ignorant of the true age of both, he declares that the morality originated in France when, in 1548, the production of mysteries was interdicted by an act of Parliament. He also wrongly supposes that the French treated "sad serious" subjects in the *moralité* and confined comedy to the *sottie,* which two forms "became, in time, the Parents of *Tragedy* and *Comedy.*" The English, however, "by jumbling them together, begot in an evil hour, that mungrel Species, unknown to Nature and Antiquity, called *Tragi-Comedy.*"

The history of fiction. Warburton's brief history of fiction first appeared as "The Editor to the Reader" in volume 4 of the 1748 edition of Samuel Richardson's *Clarissa* and was later reprinted, with Henry Fielding's name substituted for Richardson's, as a note in the edition of Pope (*P,* 4:166–69 n.).[21] Though Warburton does not explicitly confine himself to fiction in prose, it is clear that he has this limitation in mind. The genre originated, he declares, with the writing of history. Because man's curiosity about the outcome of events was normally frustrated by the brevity of human life, he turned to that "Which, by recording the principal circumstances of past facts, and laying them close together, in a continued narration, kept the mind from languishing, and gave constant exercise to its reflections." But all pleasures lead to excess. Fact was spiced by fiction "to quicken and enforce a jaded appetite," and the result was "the first barbarous

Romances, abounding with this false provocative of uncommon, extraordinary, and miraculous Adventures."

A reaction to this excess among the Spanish, the originators of romance, led to the invention of the novel. In its original form, the Spanish novel was based on plots of *"Intrigue,"* which "tho' it had indeed a kind of *Life,* it had yet, as in its infancy, nothing of *Manners."* Dissatisfaction with "the dryness of the Conduct, and want of ease in the Catastrophe" led to the invention of "the *Heroical Romances* of the *French*," which substituted *"Love* and *Honour"* for *"Life* and *Manners."* But an attempt to treat this subject matter realistically resulted in the corrupting pornography of "little amatory Novels." At last the French invented the novel proper, having "hit upon the true Secret, by which alone a deviation from strict fact, in the commerce of Man, could be really entertaining to an improved mind, or useful to promote that Improvement." This secret was "a faithful and chaste copy of *Life* and *Manners."*

On this model Richardson's *Clarissa* (in the later version, the novels of Fielding) is formed. The epistolary mode of *Clarissa* afforded the author "the only opportunity that could be had, of representing with any grace those lively and delicate impressions which *Things present* are known to make upon the minds of those affected by them." This mode is therefore superior to conventional narrative in depicting human nature, for an understanding of the immediate impressions of experience takes us "into the recesses of the Human Mind."

Originality of the histories. Nothing more need be said about the errors of fact in these essays or about the tone of overweening certainty with which the errors are paraded. What should be pointed out is that for perhaps the first time in England genuine literary history was being attempted—not just chronicles of works published or lists of writers' names, but narratives tracing the development of genres.[22] Moreover, Warburton might be said to have invented two kinds of literary history, what might be called (if the terms are not too grand for the modest performances they characterize) the sociological and the philosophical. The first is represented by the essays on romance and drama. The form and content of genres are said to be contingent on specific historical conditions: romance, on holy wars that provided subject matter and on the taste for Oriental extravagance created by contact with the East; drama, on the legal prohibition of mysteries in France, which is said to have given rise to moralities. The history of fiction, on the other hand, ignores specific historical conditions and treats the development of genres as an evolutionary process governed by the nature of the human mind. The growth of romance is attributed not to historical circumstances as in the earlier essay, but to an apparently inevitable degeneration of historical narrative caused by man's predisposition to excess and his desire for novelty. The evolution of fiction proceeds in a rising spiral, from growth to decay to growth. After each recovery, the form has ascended to a higher plane.

Like many other scholars before and since, Warburton probably misses the implications of his own originality. He does not seem to notice that he has given two different and perhaps contradictory accounts of romance, and it does not occur to him that the historical conditions by which he explains the growth of romance and drama might invite a reconsideration of the standards by which they were conventionally judged. Although in a note on Pope he writes sympathetically of Gothic architecture because he believes that its departures from classical regularity have historical causes (*P, 3*:266–69n.),[23] his standards for judging literary genres remain absolute. Romance is monstrous. Tragi-comedy is "that mungrel Species."

Interpretive Criticism

A familiar kind of twentieth-century essay in literary interpretation goes something like this. The critic paraphrases conventional interpretations of a work and dismisses them as inadequate because they fail to account for certain of the work's anomalies. Then he advances his own interpretation, a hypothesis that transforms the apparent anomalies into harmonious beauties. This hypothesis he supports by argument, citing internal or external evidence or both. He concludes by reiterating the superiority of his own hypothesis to the hypotheses of other critics and by praising the work whose rich complexity has, until this very moment, defied comprehension.

Scores of essays in this form or in variations on it are published in our learned journals every year. They are so common as to seem inevitable, as natural as weeds. Actually they are highly exotic. In America they did not begin to flourish until the 1940s, and in eighteenth-century England they did not flourish at all.[24] To my knowledge, only two eighteenth-century critics published such essays: Warburton and Richard Hurd, whom Warburton directly influenced.[25]

I hasten to explain that I am not talking about incidental interpretation in an essay otherwise devoted to making literary judgments, or about interpretation in the notes of a scholarly edition. Nor am I talking about "allegoresis," interpretation that "treats the poem as an illustration of a system of ideas existing independently of the text and its creator," a critical method that originated as early as the sixth century B.C.[26] I am talking, rather, about interpretation that advances a single hypothesis to account for the plenary meaning of a work, that claims to represent the author's conscious intention, that recognizes a historical context out of which that intention arose, and that argues at length for the validity of the hypothesis on the basis of historical evidence and internal consistency. This kind of criticism appeared for perhaps the first time in three essays in the *Divine Legation*. Before turning to these, however, it is necessary to say a few words about Warburton's more conventional *Critical and Philosophical Commentary on Mr. Pope's Essay on Man*.

The defense of the *Essay on Man*. Because Warburton's reputation in the twentieth century depends largely on his association with Pope, the defense of the *Essay on Man* is the only critical essay of his that contemporary literary scholars are likely to know. Unfortunately it is not typical of his interpretive criticism. Unlike the three essays in the *Divine Legation*, it is almost totally ahistorical and is not part of a larger theological argument, having been occasioned by Crousaz's attacks on Pope's poem. Warburton's immediate polemical purpose causes him to succumb even more completely than is his wont to the temptations of arbitrary interpretation.

The *Essay on Man* is not an explicitly Christian work. Is it therefore un-Christian or anti-Christian? This question will be raised as long as readers take an interest in Pope, but it is not likely to be definitively answered because the evidence, both internal and external, is radically ambiguous. A reader's preference for one pattern of possible meanings over another reflects his own assumptions about the nature of Christianity, about the kind of poetry Pope wrote, and, perhaps most important, about Pope's character. In a recent hostile book on Pope, for example, it is predictable long before the chapter on the *Essay on Man* that the author will dismiss as special pleading any attempt to reconcile the poem with Christian thought. "What can be Christian," he asks in response to a sympathetic analysis by Reuben Brower, "about a poem that has no reference to Christ, the Gospels, 'the mysteries of the Christian faith' and, above all, revelation?"[27] To which a defender of Pope might reply, "The intention of the poet." The absence of explicit references to doctrine, religious or other, is never decisive in literary interpretation, as the most cursory glance at the history of criticism will show.

These preliminary remarks suggest a crucial weakness in Warburton's defense. It rests on the unsupported assumption that Pope wrote as an orthodox Christian. Once this assumption is granted, many ambiguities vanish. If Pope confines himself to the doctrines of natural religion, for example, he does so not because he is a deist, but because he wants to imply that deism is inadequate. "What is this then," Warburton asks concerning Pope's depreciation of human reason in epistle 2, lines 147–54, "but an intimation that we ought to seek for a cure in that religion which only dares to profess to give it?" And again: "Mr. *Pope,* though his subject in this *Essay on Man* confines him to *natural religion* (his purpose being to vindicate God's natural dispensation to mankind against the Atheists), yet gives frequent intimations of a more sublime dispensation . . ." (*W,* 11:81, 111). These intimations may well be intended, but intention is precisely the point at issue. Given a choice between the literal sense and a Christian "intimation," a reader who doubts Pope's orthodoxy will necessarily choose the interpretation that confirms his initial assumption. Warburton's debate with Crousaz often results in this kind of stand-off. As Warburton correctly points out, Crousaz realizes that certain passages in the poem are compatible with Christian doctrine, but he refuses to read them as orthodox because he cannot believe that Pope is a Christian.[28] Though Warburton scores debater's points by impugning Crousaz's charity, he fails to see that his own assumptions about Pope's intention are no less dependent than his opponent's on a view of Pope originating outside the poem and must be defended by external evidence. But the critical essay of Warburton's that most needs a biographical and historical dimension is almost completely without it.

The essay is historically deficient in another way. It fails to place the poem in an intellectual context, a failure most evident in Warburton's remarks on the adversaries against whom the poem is allegedly directed. Pope

divide[s] his *Vindication of the Ways of God* into *two* Parts. In the *first* of which he gives *direct* answers to those objections which libertine men, on a view of the disorders arising from the perversity of the human will, have intended against Providence: And, in the *second,* he *obviates* all those objections, by a true delineation of human Nature, or *general* but exact *Map of Man;* which these objectors either not knowing, or mistaking, or else leaving (for the mad pursuit of *metaphysical entities*), have lost and bewildered themselves in a thousand foolish complaints against Providence. The *first Epistle* is employed in the management of the *first* part of this dispute; and the *three* following in the management of the *second.* (*W,* 11:24)

Warburton refers often to these adversaries and, as the quotation makes clear, regards their complaints against God as so important in Pope's scheme as to have determined the structure of the poem. One would therefore expect them to be quoted or at the very least identified, especially since a strong argument against Crousaz would have been that Pope refuted specific freethinkers. However, except for everyone's bogeyman Thomas Hobbes (*W,* 11:97), Pope's opponents are never named. It may well be that they do not exist except as creatures of Pope's and Warburton's imaginations. In the most thorough study to date of the intellectual context of the poem, Douglas White expresses considerable uncertainty about their identity and even suggests that they may include certain divines, deists, and so-called atheists who believed that "a future life is necessary to make retribution for the obvious limitations of this one."[29] Since this belief is central to the thesis of the *Divine Legation,* White's supposition would place Warburton among the adversaries of the very poem he sets out to vindicate. To my knowledge, however, White is the first reader in the two-hundred-and-fifty-year history of the poem to infer such adversaries from Pope's argument, a singularity that casts doubt, if not on the validity of the inference, at least on the clarity of the poem. But none of this excuses Warburton's failure either to name names or to concede the insubstantiality of Pope's opponents.

Another weakness of the essay is arbitrary interpretation, the forcible imposition on the poem of "a rationative rigour," to quote Maynard Mack, of which Pope was probably incapable.[30] Warburton's summary of epistle 1, intended to demonstrate the poem's "exactness of method," is typical. The poet "lays down [a] proposition as the foundation of his thesis, . . . draws from thence two consequences, . . . proceeds to confirm his thesis, . . . [and] deduces his general conclusion." To make the poem march to the beat of these propositions, theses, consequences, and deductions, Warburton must tame Pope's fractious ambiguities. He insists, for example, that in the opening sixteen lines the poet announces "the quality of his Adversaries" or "Tells us against whom he wrote, *the Atheists.*" Actually, the only line of the first sixteen that might support this interpretation is 12, which mentions "all who blindly creep or sightless soar." But Warburton does not cite this line as evidence, and he glosses it elsewhere as a reference not to Pope's adversaries, but to those who make "popular and philosophical errors concerning happiness." As his discussion of the first sixteen lines makes clear, it is epistle 1, lines 110, 114, and epistle 2, line 202, from which he derives his conception of the adversaries, which conception the systematizing theologian reads back into the beginning of the poem where he thinks it belongs (*W,* 11:24–25, 37–38; *P,* 3:4n.).

Is the essay, then, totally without redeeming value? No. It does four things well. It exposes Crousaz's errors of interpretation, it identifies the blunders of Pope's French translators, it distinguishes correctly between Leibniz and Spinoza on the one hand and Pope on the other, and it calls attention to the Christian antecedents of some of Pope's ideas. But these are routine achievements, well within the competence of many of Warburton's intellectual inferiors. If his interpretive powers were typified by the defense of the *Essay on Man,* they would not deserve further notice.

Aeneid, book 6.   The longest and most elaborate of Warburton's three important critical essays—an interpretation of *Aeneid,* book 6—is much superior to that on the *Essay on Man.* Its ostensible purpose is to clarify the social function of the Eleusinian Mysteries, but, as so often happens in the *Divine Legation,* the subsidiary argument takes on a life of its own. That it is a self-contained essay in literary interpretation is indicated by its republication as "A Dissertation on the Sixth Book of the *Aeneid*" in Joseph Warton's edition of *The Works of Virgil* (1753).

Though it centers on the sixth book, Warburton begins by advancing an interpretation of the whole poem. Virgil "aspired to make it A SYSTEM OF POLITICS, . . . as complete an institute in verse, by EXAMPLE, as the *Republics* of Plato and Tully were in prose, by PRE-CEPT" (*W,* 2:79). Among the virtues of this interpretation, according to Warburton, is its explanatory power, for much that had seemed to other critics derivative or decorative is now shown to be functional. Supernatural machinery, characterization, plot—all were designed by Virgil to illustrate his political theme.

Book 6 is said to contribute to the theme by using Aeneas's descent into the underworld as "an enigmatical representation of his

INITIATION INTO THE MYSTERIES" (*W*, 2:96). The rest of the essay is an argument, based on what Edward Gibbon aptly called "a torrent of erudition," for this interpretation.[31] The argument takes two forms. First, the logical necessity of an initiation in the poem is deduced from general principles. For example, since the mysteries, according to Warburton, were a political institution used to teach the doctrine of rewards and punishments in a future state, and since all ancient political leaders were initiated in order to set an example for the citizenry, Aeneas, an ideal political leader, had to be initiated (*W*, 2:96).

The second kind of argument involves the discovery of parallels between the circumstances of Aeneas's descent and what was known of initiation ceremonies. The Sybyl, for instance, "sustains two principal and distinct parts: that of the inspired *Priestess,* to pronounce the ORACLE; . . . and that of *Hierophant,* to conduct the Initiated through the whole CELEBRATION." The golden bough is "the *wreath of myrtle,* with which the Initiated were crowned, at the celebration of the *Mysteries.*" Aeneas's entrance into the Sybyl's cave is his initiation into the Lesser Mysteries. The personifications outside the entrance to the underworld—Grief, Cares, Diseases, Age, Fear, Famine, etc.—suggest the trials demanded of political leaders aspiring to initiation (*W*, 2:104–19). And so on for an additional fifty pages.

Much of this is easy to ridicule. For one thing, if there is a connection between book 6 and the Mysteries, Warburton has probably turned it upside down. Virgil probably used the details of initiation ceremonies to describe a descent into hell, not a descent into hell to represent initiation ceremonies. For another, Warburton has a new allegory up his sleeve to account for whatever is otherwise unaccountable (see, for instance, *W*, 2:84). His interpretation cannot be refuted, since whatever seems to contradict it never means what it says.

But for all its faults, the essay makes an important contribution to criticism of the *Aeneid.* Though Warburton's allegory of initiation is crude and may be too closely identified with Eleusis, modern scholarship vindicates the hypothesis that book 6 depends on Virgil's knowledge of initiation ceremonies. George Luck shows that Warburton's interpretation contains a core of good sense, that it cites important evidence ignored by later scholars, and that it is confirmed by evidence that Warburton could not have been aware of.[32] On the basis of recent archaeological discoveries, R. F. Paget argues that in

book 6 Virgil describes "the Great Antrum at Baiae near Avernus,
which the Ancients believed to be the Entrance to the Underworld,
with its mysterious underground Sanctuary, where initiation took
place into the Cult of the Gods of the Infernal Regions," and that he
"not only demonstrates that he, himself, was an Orphic, but gives a
graphic summary of Orphic beliefs in the underworld."[33] According
to Sir Frank Fletcher, "if, as is probable, the Mysteries involved 'a
theatrical representation of all that was believed or imagined of the
lower world, and the aspirant was conducted through the mimic
scenes of Erebus, Tartarus and Elysium,' we have a parallel in them
to the scenery and mythology of *Aeneid* VI."[34] I have placed Fletcher's
comment last, for by a cruel though unintended irony, the authority
he quotes is Edward Gibbon. Warburton goes unmentioned, though
it was he who discovered the relation between book 6 and the Mysteries, while Gibbon ridiculed the discovery in an anonymous
pamphlet.[35]

Apart from the value of its central insight, Warburton's essay is
interesting for what it has to say about methodology. As I have already pointed out, he rests his case partly on the explanatory power
of his interpretation and quotes from various critics to show that,
lacking a clear understanding of Virgil's intention, they have wrongly
identified as defects what are necessary and important contributions
to the theme. "But this key to the Æneis," he writes of his general
political interpretation, "not only clears up many passages obnoxious
to the critics, but adds infinite beauty to a great number of incidents
throughout the whole poem. . . ." His interpretation of book 6 "not
only clears up a number of difficulties, inexplicable on any other
scheme; but likewise heightens and ennobles the whole poem; for
now the episode is seen to be an essential part of the main
subject . . ." (*W*, 2:89, 160).[36] The interpretation is based on

the only Principles from which any thing reasonable can be deduced in a
piece of criticism of this nature. For, from what I had shewn was taught,
and represented in the *Mysteries*, I infer that Æneas's DESCENT INTO HELL
signifies an INITIATION; because of the exact conformity, in all circumstances, between what Virgil relates of his Hero's adventure, and what antiquity delivers concerning SHOWS and DOCTRINES of those MYSTERIES, into
which Heroes were wont to be initiated. On the contrary, had I gratuitously
supposed, without any previous knowledge of what was practiced in the
Mysteries, that the *descent* was an *initiation*, merely because Augustus (who

was shadowed under the person of Æneas) was initiated; and thence inferred, that the *Mysteries* did exhibit the same scenes which the Poet hath made *Hell* to exhibit to his Hero, my explanation had been devoid of any solid inference, as of any rational principle. (*W*, 2:167)

Of course this oversimplifies. "What antiquity delivers" concerning the Mysteries must itself be interpreted, as must the details of book 6 and the "conformity" between them and initiation ceremonies. The very hypothesis of a conformity leads to some degree of circularity, the evidence concerning the Mysteries being interpreted in the light of book 6 and vice versa. As E. D. Hirsch points out, however, no rules of interpretation can ever be fully satisfactory.[37] Warburton's "Principles" make sense as far as they go, and might be uselessly complex if taken any further. Besides, this may be the first essay in secular literary interpretation in which the critic tries to justify the logic of his method. It would be asking too much to expect him to combine an original contribution to knowledge of Virgil with a definitive theory of hermeneutics.

The essay has one additional distinction: it may be the only piece of criticism ever to have become the subject of an encomiastic poem.[38]

The Golden Ass. The second interpretive essay in the *Divine Legation* is on Lucius Apuleius's *Metamorphosis*, better known as *The Golden Ass*, a second-century narrative in Latin prose. This essay is shorter and less ambitious than that on the *Aeneid*, but it is also more generally convincing. Its ostensible purpose is to show that the Mysteries were thought "*essential* . . . to RELIGION" (*W*, 2:169).

Apuleius's intention, according to Warburton, is "to recommend PAGAN RELIGION as the only cure for *all vice whatsoever*" (*W*, 2:171). This interpretation is first supported by biographical evidence. Warburton cites what is known of Apuleius's Platonism and of his devotion to the Mysteries, both of which commitments would have made him hostile to Christianity. But there was also a personal reason for this hostility. Licinius Æmilianus, who brought suit against Apuleius on the charge that he had used magic to win the affection of the rich widow whom he had married, was a Christian. Æmilianus is nowhere so identified, but Warburton infers his Christianity from what he takes to be unmistakable insinuations in Apuleius's *Apology*. A philosophical and personal animus against Christianity thus informs the pagan piety of the fable (*W*, 2:171–80).

The internal evidence for this piety is the allegory conveyed by the tale's often frivolous and obscene subject matter. The narrator Lucius's encounter with Byrrhena, who warns him against the magician Pamphile, is a variation on Hercules' choice between Virtue and Pleasure. As a result of choosing the latter, Lucius is turned into an ass, the moral of which metamorphosis is "THAT BRUTALITY ATTENDS VICE AS IT'S [sic] PUNISHMENT" (W, 2:183–85). Lucius's adventures in the form of an ass are "the various maladies to which [Apuleius] was applying a remedy." Most of these concern "the mischiefs of unlawful love," but the episode of the priests of Cybele contrasts "CORRUPT MYSTERIES" with the "PURE RITES OF ISIS" (W, 2:187–88). The conclusion of the work—Lucius's dream of Isis, his return to human form, and his dedication to Isiac worship—represents his purification and his initiation into the Lesser and Greater Mysteries. "All this considered," Warburton concludes in this section of the essay, "we can no longer doubt but that the true design of his work was to recommend *initiation into the mysteries, in opposition to the new religion*" (W, 2:199).

This interpretation is not without its flaws. The argument for Æmilianus's Christianity is speculative at best, and since it does not in itself prove that the work is anti-Christian, it consumes more space than it is worth. Warburton also unwittingly projects Christian attitudes into Apuleius even while arguing that he is militantly pagan: "One great beauty in the conduct of the Fable," he writes, is that "every change of station, while [Lucius] remains a brute, makes his condition still more wretched and deplorable. And being now (in the *ninth* [sic for tenth] book) about to perpetrate one of the most shocking enormities; NATURE, though so deeply brutalized, REVOLTS; he abhors the idea of his projected crime; he evades his keepers; he flies to the sea-shore; and, in this solitude, begins to reflect more seriously on his lost condition. This is finely imagined; for we often see men, even after a whole life of horrors, come suddenly to themselves on the hideous aspect of some Monster-vice too frightful even for an hardened Reprobate to bear" (W, 2:188). Actually, just before the climax Lucius is more content than at any time since his transformation. The final turn of the plot is probably intended to imply that Fortune is unreliable, not that vice causes misery. Moreover, the pagan author is not nearly so shocked as the Christian critic by sexual intercourse between a woman and an ass. Lucius enjoys the experience until he is required to perform in public with a condemned murderess who is about to be thrown to the lions. It is shame and fear of the beasts, not abhorrence of bestiality, that prompt his flight.[39]

These weaknesses aside, the essay is an impressive piece of criticism. There is scarcely an important point in P. G. Walsh's two excellent chapters on the work in *The Roman Novel* that Warburton does not adumbrate, though Walsh is evidently unaware of his eighteenth-century predecessor. Like Walsh, Warburton shows that the work is both entertainment and fable; that an understanding of the historical context in which it was written helps to clarify its anti-Christian purpose; that devotion to lust and magic is the cause of a brutishness that only Isiac initiation can cure; that Psyche and her sisters in the Cupid and Psyche digression represent the Platonic division of the soul (an interpretation Walsh mentions but doubts) (*W*, 2:182–82, 172–74, 185, 202).[40] Warburton even advances an interpretation of the Cupid and Psyche tale that answers Walsh's objection to a similar interpretation by Reinhold Merkelbach, who also fails to cite Warburton. According to Merkelbach, when Psyche looks at Cupid, she is initiated into the mysteries of Isis, to whom she is thereafter devoted. Walsh dismisses this reading on the grounds that Psyche's vision of Cupid is obviously treated by Apuleius as sinful. Warburton, however, argues that Psyche's forbidden vision represents the magic of theurgy, which Apuleius opposes to lawful initiation. This interpretation anticipates Merkelbach's conclusion that an Isiac mystery has been revealed while avoiding his failure to acknowledge the sinfulness of Psyche's act (*W*, 2:203–4).[41]

Two other notable aspects of the essay should be mentioned. As in his criticism of the *Aeneid*, Warburton broaches the question of methodology. How do we know that the critic has not imposed on the tale an allegory that was never intended? We know in this instance, he declares, because Apuleius refers at the beginning of the work to Egyptian paper and Nile reeds and thus implies that the tale is "replete with Ægyptian wisdom." This answer is scarcely conclusive, though some twentieth-century scholars likewise believe that the reference to Egypt is an invitation to allegorical reading (*W*, 2:206–7).[42] The answer, however, is less important than the question, which had seldom if ever been asked by ancient, medieval, and Renaissance allegorizers.

Also interesting for its departure from earlier habits of thought is Warburton's sympathetic treatment of a work he thinks guilty of pagan "bigotry." He admires a "fine circumstance," an "artful" contrivance. Of the total design, he writes that "nothing could be better conceived, to recommend the *Mysteries,* than the idea of such a plan; or better conceived than the execution of it. In which he omits no circumstance that might be plausibly opposed to Christianity . . ." (*W,* 2:174, 185, 199). This distinction between theme and execution is a peculiarly modern exercise of the historical and aesthetic imagination, the very antithesis of the medieval and Renaissance practice of Christianizing pagan literature. I am unaware of any Christian critic before Warburton who praises the artistry of what he takes to be an attack on his own religion.

The Book of Job. The section of *The Divine Legation* on the Book of Job belongs here rather than in the chapter on theology because, while Warburton assumes that the author was divinely inspired and that the text is in all important respects uncorrupted, he treats the book as a work of secular fiction. The deficiencies of his interpretation derive not from Christian piety but from ignorance. He did not know Hebrew, and he wrote before the Higher Criticism demonstrated that certain books of the Bible were formed by combining different and sometimes contradictory sources. Naturally he lacked the knowledge of the ancient Near East that only nineteenth- and twentieth-century philology and archeology could provide. These limitations admitted, however, his interpretation is more astute than has generally been recognized and seems in some ways more up to date than those of later commentators who did not labor under his disadvantages.

The purpose of the essay is to show that the Book of Job does not teach a future state of rewards and punishments. "In the order of this discourse therefore," Warburton announces,

I shall inquire,
    I.   What kind of composition the book of Job really is.
   II.   In what age it was written. And,
  III.   Who was its Author. (*W,* 5:299)

His answer to the first question is that the work is a drama. By this he means not only that it differs from narrative but that it is a fiction, a work of the imagination. He cites as evidence the author's use of verse, his richly metaphorical style, and the improbable psychology of his characters. Nobody can seriously believe, Warburton argues, that three men, having come to comfort a mourning friend and having joined him in silent grief for seven days and seven nights, would then "wrangle, and contradict him in every word he spoke; and this without the least softening of friendship; but with all the fierceness and acrimony of Disputants contending for a victory." If, however, the work is a drama and the drama an allegory, this strange behavior can be taken as a requirement of plot and theme. The author's treatment of God is also evidence of the fictionality of the work. God's intervention at the end of the book is clearly a *deus ex machina,* but He answers none of the questions raised by the disputants. The reason is that "the sacred Writer was no wiser when he spoke poetically in the Person of God, than when he spoke in the person of Job or his friends." God is merely a character in the play (*W,* 5:299–304).

Warburton's answer to the second question is that "the BOOK OF JOB was written some time between the return [from captivity], and the thorough settlement of the Jews in their own country." Against the argument that the book contains no reference to the laws of Moses, he cites the requirements of artistic decorum and the existence of various anachronisms that suggest a date of composition much later than the time of the dramatic action. He places the work not long after the return from captivity because, he thinks, the question on which the drama turns—the nature of God's justice—makes sense only at this moment in Jewish history. Earlier, the Jews had known that they lived under an extraordinary providence; later, they knew that they did not. It was only when the extraordinary providence was first withdrawn that the question of God's justice was sufficiently vexed to provide the basis of a dramatic conflict (*W,* 5:306–28).

The book, Warburton continues, is an allegory written to console the Jews for the apparent loss of God's favor. Job represents the Jewish people at the time of the return from captivity. His wife is a pagan and serves as a warning against intermarriage. The three friends represent Sanbalat, Tobiah, and Gesham, enemies of the Jewish nation. Satan's "assault upon Job [is] that very attack which, the Prophet Zechariah tells us, Satan made, at this time, on the PEOPLE." And Elihu represents the poet himself (*W,* 5:328–69).

As for the final question, the identity of the poet, Warburton replies that he was none other than Ezra, "one of the most eminent of *God's* prophets," who in his authorship of the work was divinely inspired (*W,* 5:369–70).

The attribution of the book to Ezra is a blunder that has deprived Warburton's essay of the respect it deserves. When in 1765 he goaded Robert Lowth, author of *Lectures on the Sacred Poetry of the Hebrews,* into published debate on the subject, he left himself vulnerable to the attack of a specialist in Hebrew who was able to expose his linguistic ignorance. But Lowth's gift for satire was more damaging than his scholarship. By means of elegant *ad hominem* ironies at the expense of Warburton's notorious truculence in literary controversy, he created a nearly indestructible image of his adversary as a blustering ignoramus.[43] So complete was his triumph that everyone seems to have overlooked Warburton's partial vindication by later scholarship. No twentieth-century authority would take seriously Lowth's view that Job "is the most ancient of all the sacred books" and that "whoever could suppose it written after the Babylonish captivity, would fall little short of the error of Hardouin, who ascribed the golden verses of Virgil, Horace, &c. to the *iron age* of monkish pedantry and ignorance."[44] Warburton's dating, on the other hand, has the support of much recent scholarship, as does his argument that the issue of God's providence indicates the work's early post-exilic origin.[45] One twentieth-century scholar, Denis Baly, has independently advanced an allegorical interpretation similar to Warburton's:

It seems probable that the date of the book in its original form is fairly soon after the return from Exile, somewhere toward the end of the sixth century or beginning of the fifth, and that the well-known legendary figure of Job is used to represent the exiled people of Judah, who had been overwhelmed by catastrophe, as drastic and complete as had been the disasters that happened to Job.[46]

Baly does not develop this reading and might hesitate to follow Warburton in finding an allegorical counterpart for each of the characters besides Job. But Warburton's overingenuity should not obscure his shrewdness in inferring the date of the work from the nature of its theme.

Even his overingenuity is in harmony with twentieth-century exegesis—not, I hasten to add, because recent biblical scholarship necessarily concocts fantastic interpretations, but because, in correcting the excesses of nineteenth-century theories of multiple sources, twentieth-century scholars must find their own unifying hypotheses.[47] Since they make use of emendation and the deletion and transposition of verses, practices that Warburton's conception of the sacred text did not permit, their interpretations need not be as elaborate as his, which is explicitly intended to reconcile every apparent contradiction that the Book of Job was known to contain. The inconsistency between Job's reputation for patience and his nearly blasphemous complaints shows "That some other Character, [is] shadowed under that of Job . . ." (*W*, 5:331). Likewise, "The great point which Job so much insists upon throughout the whole book is his *innocence:* and yet, to our surprise, we hear him, in one place, thus expostulating with GOD: *Thou writest bitter things against me, and makest me to possess the* INIQUITIES OF MY YOUTH. This can be accounted for no otherwise than by understanding it of the PEOPLE: whose repeated iniquities on their first coming out of Egypt, were in every Age remembered, and punished on their Posterity" (*W*, 5:331). Every allegorical identification, so seemingly arbitrary in my bald summary above, serves a similar unifying function. The "chief advantage" of his all-inclusive interpretation, he declares, is that "it renders one of the most difficult and obscure books in the whole Canon, the most easy and intelligible; reconciles all the characters to Nature, all the arguments to Logic, and all the doctrines to the course and order of God's Dispensations." It is "able to lay open and unfold the whole conduct of the Poem upon one entire, perfect, elegant and noble plan . . ." (*W*, 5:371, 383). One need not accept this estimate of Warburton's achievement to appreciate the difficulty of the problem that he tries to solve, or to admire the learning and intelligence that he brings to the attempt.

Practice versus Theory

Warburton never makes explicit or generalizes the radical implications of his interpretive criticism. On expressive grounds he praises Virgil for combining the structures of *The Iliad* and *The Odyssey,* and the author of the Book of Job for creating an unrealistic, allegorical, almost actionless drama. Yet, having shown in two important instances that form follows theme, he overlooks the potential fruitfulness of his own discovery and lapses into the conventionalities of the theoretical criticism examined at the beginning of the chapter. It is worth remarking that Pope's praise of Warburton as a critic was recorded by Joseph Spence in 1742. Apart from the defense of the *Essay on Man* and some commentary on Spenser and Shakespeare, the interpretive essays in the *Divine Legation* were at that time the only criticism by Warburton that Pope could have read.

Chapter Four

The Editor

The Edition of Shakespeare

Reluctant enthusiasm. Warburton worked at Shakespeare off and on for at least forty years. By 1726 he had already devised a theory about Shakespeare's knowledge of the ancients, and in 1729 he began a voluminous Shakespearean correspondence with Lewis Theobald that lasted until 1736. When he broke with Theobald, he was already engaged in a similar correspondence with Sir Thomas Hanmer, this one lasting until 1739. In this year he published commentary on Shakespeare in the English translation of Bayle's *Dictionary,* and in the following year in the *History of the Works of the Learned.* He was, he told Thomas Birch in September 1739, "at every leisure hour, transcribing all my notes and emendations fair into books, to fit them for the press," and he must have had to revise them after the publication of Theobald's *Shakespeare* of 1740, from which his own edition was printed.[1] He worked on the anonymously edited *Shakespear* of 1745, and his own edition of 1747 showed evidence of having been labored over and revised even as it went to press. In his personal copy he continued to enter revisions until at least 1767.[2]

But he was most reluctant to confess his commitment to Shakespearean scholarship. In his preface he called himself a "Critic by Profession" but falsely declared that the edition was the product of "my younger amusements, when, many years ago, I used to turn over these sort of Writers to unbend myself from more serious applications . . ." (*S,* 1:viii, xix). The source of this ambivalence was probably his rigoristic view of clerical responsibility. In a charge he urged the clergy of Gloucester to cultivate learning but was careful to explain that he meant only "those studies that relate immediately to your ministry." To Richard Hurd he expressed the hope that the poet and clergyman William Mason would divest himself of "those idle baggages [that is, his poetry], after his sacred espousals," and speaking of the Reverend John Brown's having arranged for the production of a play, he lamented that "either these *unrewarding times,* or his *love of poetry,* or his *love of money,* should have made him overlook the duty of a Clergyman in these times, and the dignity of a Clergyman in all times, to make connexions with Players" (*W,* 9:374).[3] This contempt for actors is more than mere snobbery. Almost certainly he never saw a play of Shakespeare performed. Indeed, his religious scruples were such that he may never have entered a theater.[4] Why, then, did he take on the laborious, time-consuming task of editing the plays?

The challenge of Shakespeare. In a lifetime of research, the most gifted scholar of the early eighteenth century could not have acquired a fraction of the knowledge of Shakespeare that is now accessible to any undergraduate. By 1700 Elizabethan England seemed more remote than ancient Rome. There were excellent Latin dictionaries but no satisfactory dictionaries of English, and much of Shakespeare's vocabulary was obsolete and no longer understood. There were Latin grammars but no grammars of Elizabethan English, which, differing from eighteenth-century English, often looked barbarous. Editions of Latin classics abounded, but Elizabethan works were scarce and costly, and there were no great public libraries. If we can imagine meeting Shakespeare for the first time in a seventeenth-century edition, lacking the aid of those notes and glossaries and handbooks we now take for granted, we can begin to appreciate the obstacles that stood in the way of the common reader's understanding and that challenged both scholars and dilettantes to produce a readable and accurate edition.

This task, difficult enough under the circumstances, was complicated by the combined effects of three other conditions: the complex history of Shakespeare's text, the state of bibliographical knowledge, and the rage for emendation that afflicted even the most conservative scholars of the period.

No manuscript of Shakespeare's plays has survived. The study of the text must begin with the First Folio of 1623, the collection brought together by Shakespeare's friends and fellow actors John Heminge and Henry Condell. Of the thirty-six plays that the Folio contains, eighteen had never before been printed, twelve had been printed as quartos in a different form, and six had been printed as quartos in a form not substantially different from that in the Folio. Many of the quartos had been reprinted before 1623 (sometimes with false publication dates), and the Folio itself was reprinted in 1632, 1663, and 1685. To the 1663 and 1685 editions were added seven new plays, of which only *Pericles* is now accepted as Shakespeare's.

The early eighteenth-century editors—Nicholas Rowe, Pope, Theobald, Hanmer, and Warburton—were not aware of all of the quartos, but they were aware of a sufficient number to realize that the printing history was complicated. What they failed to realize is that careful distinctions must be made between good and bad texts. Pope correctly identified the first editions of *A Midsummer Night's Dream* and the two parts of *Henry IV* as better than average, but for the most part the only distinctions he acknowledged were between bad and worse. Believing that the First Folio was inferior to all of the quartos, for example, he removed to the bottom of the page lines from the Folio *Romeo and Juliet* because they did not appear in the bad quarto of 1597. On the basis of date alone, Theobald divided the texts into three classes: "Editions of Authority" (the First and Second Folios, and all texts published before 1623), "Editions of Middle Authority" (other seventeenth-century editions), and "Editions of No Authority" (eighteenth-century editions). He recognized no differences between texts in the first class, however, implying in his preface that the causes of corruption had made all of the early editions equally unreliable.[5] This failure to distinguish between degrees of reliability helped to encourage textual license. An editor felt free to choose a variant reading he happened to like without worrying about the authority of the text he found it in. He even felt free to reject a reading common to all of the texts and substitute one of his own.

Also contributing to editorial license was the editors' failure to distinguish between a "polygenous" and a "monogenous" series. Different manuscripts of the same classical work are normally part of a polygenous series, that is, they descend by different routes from an ancient lost original. An editor must treat all the texts in a polygenous group as of equal authority, weighing the possibility that any reading may be derived from the original manuscript. Printed texts, however, are normally part of a monogenous series, that is, the second edition is printed from the first, the third from the second, and so on. This means that all editions after the first lack textual authority unless it can be shown that changes in the later editions were made by the author or derived from his manuscript. Possibly because they were used to the methods of classical scholarship, the early editors treated Shakespeare's texts as if they belonged to a polygenous series. A few early texts may have been printed from different Shakespeare manuscripts of equal authority, but these exceptions, unknown to the eighteenth-century editors in any case, would not have justified the blanket assumption that one text is as good as another. Yet this is the assumption that each editor evidently made. Instead of printing from an early text that was free of accumulated errors and "corrections," Rowe printed from the Folio of 1685, Pope printed from Rowe, Theobald and Hanmer printed from Pope, and Warburton printed from Theobald. Each editor adopted many of his predecessors' errors and emendations while introducing new ones of his own.[6]

Bibiliographical ignorance also encouraged, and was encouraged by, a rage for conjectural emendation, the replacement of an alleged textual corruption by a word or phrase that an editor believes—on logical, linguistic, or metrical grounds—to be what the author actually wrote. Richard Bentley's success at emending notoriously corrupt Greek texts had made the method so fashionable that Bentley himself could not resist misapplying it. In 1732 he published an edition of *Paradise Lost* containing more than a thousand emendations (including the immortal "transpicuous gloom" for Milton's "darkness visible").[7] Though extreme, this edition was symptomatic. "Wholesale emendation was indeed so common an editorial practice," R. G. Moyles observes of the early eighteenth century, "that should one reproduce a composite passage from *Paradise Lost,* incorporating all early corruptions and emendations, the passage would be wholly unrecognizable as being Milton's."[8]

The appeals of conjectural emendation are many. There is the challenge of the guessing game: How is the editor to repair an obvious corruption? There is the challenge of debate: How is he to defend the change?[9] There is the challenge of detection: How is he to recognize, among multitudes of seemingly genuine words, the hundreds of impostors that must surely have stolen into the text during the course of its transmission? To justify the discovery of such impostors in *Paradise Lost,* Bentley went so far as to invent an editor who, taking advantage of Milton's blindness, had added to the first edition a number of his own lines.[10] No such fiction was needed by the editors of Shakespeare because the printed text was universally believed to be based not on the author's manuscript but on hopelessly garbled playhouse copies. Thus arose a climate of textual despair in which emendatory extravagance could flourish. "Those who fancied that

Shakespeare's manuscripts had been left to the care of door-keepers and prompters," Peter Alexander remarks, "were bolder in the exercise of conjecture than those can be who believe that in many instances the text they examine was printed from Shakespeare's own manuscript."[11] Nor were these boldly conjecturing editors likely to question the conventional bibliographical wisdom when it legitimized the method they were all too eager to use.

These, then, were the circumstances that tempted Warburton to neglect theology for Shakespeare. To restore the greatest of English poets to his original purity was to win certain renown as a scholar. But to do so by means of conjectural emendation—this was to share in the glory of poetic creation.

Contents of the edition. In the contents of the *Shakespear,* Warburton for the most part imitates his eighteenth-century predecessors. He follows (1) Pope in calling attention to memorable passages by means of quotation marks, and in printing an "Index of the Characters, Sentiments, Similies, Speeches, and Descriptions"; (2) Pope and Theobald in printing a table of editions allegedly consulted and collated; (3) Pope and Hanmer in printing Rowe's life of Shakespeare and Ben Jonson's poem on Shakespeare from the First Folio; and (4) Hanmer in printing Pope's preface.

Only Warburton's preface and notes need extended discussion, but a preliminary word may be said about one curious innovation—a list of tragedies and comedies, each group divided into four classes, and each play numbered according to Warburton's estimate of its merit relative to other plays in the same class. Lacking an explicit rationale, these rankings have little value apart from the glimpse they afford of a taste in Shakespeare significantly different from that of the twentieth century. The biggest surprises are the grouping of histories with tragedies (possibly because history plays were not recognized as a kind by the ancients), the high estimate of both parts of *Henry IV* (supreme among the "tragedies"), and the low estimates of *Antony and Cleopatra* (next to last in class 2) and *Romeo and Juliet* (last in class 3). Possibly the subject matter of the two latter—romantic love—accounts for Warburton's coolness, but this is speculation. He does not reveal in the notes greater or lesser enthusiasm for any of the plays, nor is there a correlation between the amount of commentary and the position of a play in the hierarchy. Ironically, the classification of the plays may have provided a model for Joseph Warton's classification of English poets in his *Essay on the Genius and Writings of Pope*—a classification designed, much to Warburton's annoyance, to place Pope in the second rank (*S*, 1 :sig. D8ᵛ-E1ʳ). [12]

An eighteenth-century preface to Shakespeare was almost as conventional as the contents of the edition it introduced. All or most of the following topics were treated, though in varying orders and degrees of emphasis: the extent of Shakespeare's learning, his beauties and blemishes, his extraordinary imagination and untutored genius, the causes of the corruption of the text, the inadequacies of previous editions, the duties of an editor, and the present editor's performance of his duties. [13] Warburton treats most of these topics and implies by his silence on the others his agreement with the treatment of them in the reprinted preface by Pope.

The argument of the preface goes as follows. Shakespeare relied on posterity not only to judge his work soundly but to restore to original purity what "Doorkeepers and Prompters" had defiled. The first printers failing to realize that the plays had to be stripped of "extraneous Scurf," it was not until the advent of Nicholas Rowe, a mere poet, that an editor was employed to improve the text. Bumbling Rowe was followed by Pope, who performed remarkably well for an amateur, and Pope was followed by Theobald and Hanmer, who "left their Author in ten times a worse Condition than they found him," and who "separately possessed those two Qualities which, more than any other, have contributed to bring the Art of Criticism into disrepute, *Dulness of Apprehension,* and *Extravagance of Conjecture*" (*S,* 1:vi–xiii).

The duties of an editor are "to correct the faulty Text; to remark the Peculiarities of Language; to illustrate obscure Allusions; and to explain the Beauties and Defects of Sentiment or Composition." All of this Warburton has done. His notes, therefore, take in "the whole Compass of Criticism." From occasional remarks on the nature of textual criticism, the reader will be able to derive a *"body of Canons"* which the editor had once intended to provide "in form." His occasional definitions of Shakespeare's words will take the place of "a general alphabetic *Glossary,*" and his occasional remarks on Shakespeare's beauties and faults will make unnecessary a "Character" of the poet "in a continued discourse" (*S,* 1:vi–xix).

In the remainder of the preface, Warburton specifies the occasion of the edition ("the conduct of the two last Editors, and the persuasions of dear Mr. POPE"); thanks the "Proprietors" (presumably the Tonson firm, which owned the copyright) for making the edition pos-

sible, and praises booksellers in general; and defends himself against
the anticipated charge that editing Shakespeare is unseemly work for
a clergyman. He cites in his own defense the precedent of Chry-
sostom's reputed love of Aristophanes, and—with ironic intent—the
importance implicitly accorded Shakespeare by Oxford University's
lavish printing of the edition by Hanmer. Apart from precedent,
there is "the reason of the thing." Shakespeare is supreme at teaching
the most important of all secular lessons, knowledge of human nature, and "to engage the Reader's due attention to it, hath been one
of the principal objects of this Edition." Moreover, the study of one's
native language is profoundly important, as the greatest of both the
ancients and the moderns testify. But there is no standard English
grammar or dictionary because the works of the most distinguished
English writers, from which a grammar and dictionary must be
drawn, have never been authoritatively edited. That this deficiency is
being repaired is suggested by the promise of new editions of Fletcher
and Milton, though most scholars still favor the classical languages.
On the other hand, classical scholarship should not be denigrated.
The West owes a debt of gratitude to "such as *Muretus, Scaliger, Ca-
saubon, Salmasius, Spanheim, Bentley,*" whose "deathless labours" preserved the achievements of the Renaissance. The essay concludes with
Warburton's favorite maxim from Thomas Hobbes, which, he declares, he would fix to the brow of every grammarian: "WORDS ARE
THE MONEY OF FOOLS, AND THE COUNTERS OF WISE MEN" (*S,*
1:xix–xxviii).

Excluding the essay on romance at the end of *Love's Labour's Lost*
and an essay on "Æneas's tale to Dido" (*Hamlet,* 2. 2. 454–541) at
the end of *Hamlet,* the notes to the plays number 2,669. Of these,
511 are attributed to commentators other than Warburton: 250 to
Pope, 116 to Theobald, 110 to Hanmer, 25 to Styan Thirlby, 2 to
Martin Folkes, 1 to Nicholas Hardinge, 2 to Hawley Bishop, and 3
to "Anonymous," one of these from Samuel Johnson's *Observations on
Macbeth* (*S,* 6:396n. 3).[14] Though all of the notes by Pope and a few
by Theobald and Hanmer are reprinted verbatim, most of the notes
by other commentators consist only of an emendation that Warburton
accepts and the name of its author, no justification for the change
being included.

The rest of the notes—2,158—are Warburton's. If these are classified according to his conception of the four duties of an editor, 941

concern the text, 850 concern language, 209 concern allusions, 148 concern praise or blame, and 10 concern miscellaneous matters that cannot be forced into any of the other categories. The numbers may be misleading, since as many as half of the notes treat two or more topics and might reasonably be classified differently. Thus there is more judicial criticism than the figure 148 seems to indicate, for I have included in this category only such notes as are devoted exclusively, or almost exclusively, to praise or blame. On the other hand, there is less textual criticism than the number 941 would imply because I have placed in this category any note, however varied its subject matter, that emends the text, questions the authenticity of a line, or refers to a folio or quarto reading. Though Warburton is justifiably notorious for emendatory extravagance, it should be noticed that, by the most liberal estimate, only about 43 percent of his notes are textual, and many of these contain no emendations.

Faults of the edition.   Allardyce Nicoll discovers in all eighteenth-century editors of Shakespeare "a note of recrimination," "a tone of triumph and satirical bitterness," "a querulous note";[15] and while this is scarcely true of Hanmer and Johnson, it is more or less true of the others, and incontestably true of Warburton. He insures the reader's hostility by adopting an attitude of insufferable self-confidence, insisting even on the title page that "The Genuine Text . . . is here settled: Being restored from the Blunders of the first Editors, and the Interpolations of the two Last." The same certainty of manner pervades the preface. Nowhere does Warburton admit the complexity of the textual problem or concede the possibility of reasonable disagreement about the accuracy of his emendations or the soundness of his opinions. When he boasts that his notes "take in the whole Compass of Criticism" and that his occasional remarks on textual criticism will serve for a "body of Canons," he challenges every reader to give the lie to his pretensions. Thomas Edwards's immensely popular *The Canons of Criticism,* in which critical principles are ironically derived from the most outrageous of Warburton's notes, is only one expression of the almost universal scorn he managed to provoke.[16] Another, for obvious reasons less well known, is the marginalia in the *Shakespear* belonging to the irascible Styan Thirlby. In support of the assertion that Pope had urged him to publish, Warburton tells the reader in a footnote to "See his letters to me," though these had never been published. Next to this note Thirlby writes in exasperation, "You might as well have said see my arse in a band box." Elsewhere he scrawls such comments as "ridiculous," "monstrous," "ass," "Stupid wretch," "fool," and "let me not let a fart."[17]

If the tone of the preface prepares the reader to reject the commentary, the tone of the commentary distracts him from the plays. Turning to a note for enlightenment, he may find instead a continuation from the preface of uncharitable attacks on the defenseless Theobald and Hanmer, or a characterization of luminous Shakespearean lines as "stark nonsense," "strange nonsense," "intolerable nonsense," "sad nonsense," "absolute nonsense," "miserable nonsense." It is as if during the performance of a play the producer kept thrusting himself to center stage to berate his theatrical rivals and abuse the script.

Warburton's most notorious fault is gratuitous emendation, and in this too he is not alone. Theobald, the best of the early eighteenth-century editors, had only about 37 percent of his 429 emendations incorporated in the standard nineteenth-century Shakespeare, the Globe edition, and twentieth-century editors, being more conservative than their predecessors, must have reduced that percentage even further.[18] An emendation by Benjamin Heath, one of Warburton's severest eighteenth-century critics, will place the latter's extravagance in perspective. In *As You Like It* (3. 2. 204), Rosalind exclaims, "Good my complexion!" Warburton takes the expression to mean "*Hold good my complexion,* i.e., let me not blush"—a gloss that is still widely accepted. But Heath rejects Warburton's reading on the grounds that there is no precedent for using "good" to mean "hold good" and that Rosalind has no cause to blush anyway. What Shakespeare really wrote, he suggests, is "Good my coz perplexer."[19] One is reminded of the seventeenth-century naturalist who rejected the popular belief that birds hibernate under water and then argued that they fly to the moon.[20]

Still, however frequent their flights of fancy, some reserve of tact or common sense keeps the other Shakespearean commentators from exploiting to the full the license that their bibliographical theory permits. In sustained lunacy, therefore, Warburton is without a rival. W. W. Greg declares that one characteristic of good emendations is that their rightness is immediately apparent to qualified readers.[21] If the contrary is true—that the wrongness of bad emendations is also immediately apparent—the following need no comment: *The Merry Wives of Windsor,* 5. 5. 43: "You orphan heirs of fixed destiny" ("You *ouphen*-heirs"); *The Merchant of Venice,* 2. 6. 6: "O, ten times faster

Venus' pigeons fly" ("Venus' *Widgeons* fly"); *As You Like It,* 2. 7. 177–78: "Thy tooth is not so keen/Because thou art not seen" ("Because thou art not *sheen*"); *Love's Labour's Lost,* 4. 3. 148: "How will he triumph, leap and laugh at it!" ("triumph, *geap,* and laugh at it"); *All's Well that Ends Well,* 1. 1. 217–18: "but the composition that your valour and fear makes in you is a virtue of a good wing" ("a virtue of a good *ming*"); ibid., 2. 1. 201: "With any branch or image of thy state" ("or *impage* of thy state"); *Cymbeline,* 3. 4. 51–52: "Some jay of Italy/Whose mother was her painting" ("Whose *meether* was her painting").[22]

One thing can be said for these emendations. They are consistent with the axiom that a scribe or compositor is more likely to mistake an unfamiliar word for a familiar one than vice versa. Indeed, some of Warburton's substitutions are so unfamiliar as to invite the suspicion that they are here being used for the first time in the history of the language. "Geap," "impage," and "meether," for example, do not seem to have found their way into dictionaries. On the other hand, "ming" is a genuine English word. It really is. It even means what Warburton says it does—a mixture. The *Oxford English Dictionary,* which cites no instance before 1823, may have to be corrected. But though Warburton might have heard the word spoken in, say, Nottinghamshire dialect, there is no evidence for his assertion that it was "common to *Shakespear* and the writers of this age." His note is evidently a ming of fact and fiction.

The fiction raises questions about his scholarly, as opposed to his critical, reliability. In some respects he is no more untrustworthy than his predecessors. They falsely claim to have collated all editions; so does he. They silently appropriate others' work; so does he. In other respects, however, he carries fraud to lengths undreamed of in their philology.

He is unscrupulous, for instance, in his attempts to discredit Theobald. Lounsbury points out that in 1730 Theobald asked Warburton if he could identify the pirate Bargulus mentioned in *Henry VI,* part 2 (4. 1. 108), or Abradas, who appears in the quarto. Evidently he could not, so in the edition of 1733 Theobald has to confess his ignorance. In 1747, having discovered that Bargulus is mentioned by Cicero, Warburton sneers, "Mr. *Theobald* says, *This wight I have not been able to trace, or discover from what legend our author derived his acquaintance with him.* And yet he is to be met with in *Tully's Offices. . . .*" Actually Theobald writes "these wights," meaning both Bargulus and

Abradas, but since Warburton knows nothing of Abradas either, he changes Theobald's plural to a singular.[23] Another instance: In his personal copy of the edition of 1733, next to Theobald's note emending "Castle" to "Casque" in *Titus Andronicus* (3. 1. 170), Warburton prints his name in ink, evidently claiming credit for at least part of the note. In his own edition, however, he contemptuously rejects it and ridicules Theobald for failing to realize that "castle" is a type of helmet.[24]

Merits of the edition.   Deficient in both common sense and integrity, Warburton as an editor of Shakespeare can be consigned to a decent, and almost total, obscurity. Almost total. For, as David Nichol Smith observes, "A man of his intellectual acquirements could not bring out an edition that was wholly bad."[25]

To begin with, except for the anonymously edited *Shakespear* of 1745, the purpose of which was to point out Hanmer's silent appropriation of others' work, Warburton's edition is the first to try to give credit to earlier editors for their emendations and glosses.[26] Though Warburton is not thorough enough to escape suspicions of plagiarism, he is more generous with attributions than has usually been acknowledged. Lounsbury understates when he says that Warburton "occasionally" gives Theobald credit for emendations.[27] He gives Theobald credit in 116 notes, a total that does not include those that acknowledge his emendations by attacking them.

Warburton is also the first editor to include in his commentary analysis of character and interpretation that goes beyond individual words or lines.[28] The judicial criticism that is the glory of Johnson's edition owes something to this precedent, without which Johnson might have confined himself to textual commentary in the manner of Theobald.

Warburton's judicial criticism is never brilliant, but it is often sensible and sometimes illuminating. An essay appended to *Hamlet*—on "Æneas's tale to Dido" (2. 2. 454–541)—may be the finest he ever wrote. Its clarity of style and dignified objectivity of tone are exemplified by the opening paragraph:

The two greatest Poets of this and the last age, Mr. *Dryden,* in the preface to *Troilus and Cressida,* and Mr. *Pope,* in his note on this place, have concurred in thinking that *Shakespear* produced this long passage with design to ridicule and expose the bombast of the Play, from whence it was taken; and that *Hamlet's* commendation of it is purely ironical. This is become the general opinion. I think just otherwise; and that it was given with commendation to upbraid the false taste of the audience of that time, which would not suffer them to do justice to the simplicity and sublime of this production. And I reason, First, From the Character *Hamlet* gives of the Play, from whence the passage is taken. Secondly, From the passage itself. And Thirdly, From the effect it had on the audience. (*S,* 8:267–72)

Like the literary essays in the *Divine Legation,* this has the flavor of twentieth-century interpretive criticism and, except for its eighteenth-century language, would not seem out of place in the most recent scholarly journal.

Warburton's comments on character are seldom intended to subsume all of the evidence under a single generalization. They aim instead to show what a passage reveals about the psychology of the speaker and about Shakespeare's understanding of human nature. Of a passage in Hal's rejection of Falstaff (*Henry IV,* part 2, 5. 5. 57–59) he writes:

Nature is highly touched in this passage. The king, having shaken off his vanities, schools his old companion for his follies with great severity: he assumes the air of a preacher; bids him fall to his *prayers,* seek *grace,* and leave *gormandizing.* But that word unluckily presenting him with a pleasant idea, he cannot forbear pursuing it. *Know, the Grave doth gape for thee thrice wider,* &c. and is just falling back into Hal by a humourous allusion to *Falstaff's* bulk; but he perceives it immediately, and fearing Sir *John* should take the advantage of it, checks both himself and the knight, with
    Reply not to me with a fool-born jest;
and so resumes the thread of his discourse, and goes moralizing to the end of the chapter. Thus the poet copies nature with great skill, and shews us how apt men are to fall back into their old customs, when the change is not made by degrees, and brought into a habit, but determined of at once on the motives of honour, interest or reason. (*S,* 4:311, n. 3)

A note on the character of Polonius provoked a reply by Johnson, and though of the two interpretations Warburton's is the less elegant, it also depends less on bare assertion. Johnson's Polonius is a complex, even sympathetic figure, an old man "who knows that his mind was once strong, and knows not that it is become weak," one in whom "dotage encroach[es] upon wisdom." But Warburton's Polonius was never wise. He is too weak to be the author of [the precepts he speaks], though he was pedant enough to have met with them in his reading, and fop enough to get them by heart and retail them for his own. And this the poet has finely shewn us was the case, where, in the middle of Polonius's instructions to his servant, he makes him, tho' without having received any interruption, forget his lesson, and say,

> *And then, Sir, does he this;*
> *He does—what was I about to say?*
> *I was about to say something—Where did I leave?—*

The servant replies,

> *At,* closes in the consequence.

This sets Polonius right . . . which shews they were words got by heart which he was repeating. Otherwise *closes in the consequences,* which conveyes no particular idea of the subject he was upon, could never have made him recollect where he broke off.[29]

Johnson's reading is subtle and humane, but Warburton's seems closer to the text.

Warburton's scholarship is often as sensible as his criticism. Though Theobald is usually given the credit, to Warburton belongs the discovery that Edgar's mad speeches in *King Lear* allude to Bishop Samuel Harsnet's *Declaration of Egregious Popish Impostures.*[30] T. W. Baldwin, the distinguished twentieth-century authority on Shakespeare's classical learning, cites approvingly Warburton's identification of an allusion to Juvenal in *Hamlet* (2. 2. 198) and his recognition of Cicero's *Tusculan Disputations* as the source of a speech in *Measure for Measure.*[31] His identification of an allusion to Mary Queen of Scots in *A Midsummer Night's Dream* (2. 1. 148–68), accepted by some scholars and rejected by others, is partly supported by historical evidence of which he was unaware (*S,* 1:113–15, n. 2).[32] His multifarious learning also contributes to reasonable emendations. All editions of *Timon of Athens* prior to Warburton's follow the Folio at 4. 3. 87–88, where Timon says, "bring down rose-cheeked youth/To the Fubfast and the diet." Recognizing from his reading in the history of medicine an allusion to a cure for venereal disease in which the patient was made to sweat in a tub, Warburton rightly changes "Fubfast" to "Tub-fast" (*S,* 6:209, n. 4).

Other obscurities he clarifies or emends by native wit alone. A line in *King Lear,* "This night wherein the cub-drawn bear would couch" (3. 1. 12), he explains, means "that even hunger, and the support of its young, would not force the bear to leave its den in such a night," the term "cub-drawn" signifying that the bear's "dugs are drawn dry by its young." In *As You Like It,* the Clown says, "When a man's verses cannot be understood, nor a man's good Wit seconded with the forward child, Understanding; it strikes a man more dead than a great reckoning, in a little room" (3. 3. 12–15). "A great reckoning in a little room," Warburton observes, "implies that the entertainment was mean, and the bill extravagant. . . . When men are joking together in a merry humour, all are disposed to laugh. One of the company says a good thing; the jest is not taken; all are silent, and he who said it, quite confounded. This is compared to a tavern jollity interrupted by the coming in of a *great reckoning*" (*S,* 6:70, n. 3; 2:346, n. 2). Warburton's most famous emendation is of *Hamlet,* 2. 2. 182, where he changes "a good kissing carrion" to "a God, kissing carrion." Though a case can be made for the original reading, the emendation is still widely accepted and is said by Johnson to be one "which almost sets the critick on a level with the author," the highest praise, perhaps, that any editor of Shakespeare has ever received (*S,* 8:165–66, n. 6).[33]

Soon after the *Sheakespear* appeared, the Dublin printer Augustus Long published an unauthorized edition of *As You Like It* based on Warburton's text and containing a selection of his notes. I have not seen this edition, but I am more than willing to credit the opinion of La Tourette Stockwell that Long's excisions and condensations effect an enormous improvement.[34] Warburton might have produced one of the most important eighteenth-century editions of Shakespeare if he had brought to the work, along with his learning and intelligence, the shrewd common sense of a Dublin pirate.

The Edition of Pope

Delay in publication. Pope died on 30 May 1744, leaving to Warburton "the property of all such of my works already printed, as he hath written, or shall write commentaries or notes upon, and which I have not otherwise disposed of, or alienated; and all the profits which shall arise after my death from such editions as he shall publish without future alterations."[35] Individual poems edited by

Warburton appeared during the forties, but the *Works*—in nine octavo volumes, lacking the translations of Homer but containing some of the prose and Pope's letters—did not appear until June 1751.

This delay can be attributed in part to Warburton's work on other projects, including the *Shakespear* and *Julian,* but another cause may have been legal complications involving unsold volumes of Pope's poems, including the so-called "death-bed edition" of the *Moral Essays,* which Pope and Warburton had been preparing since the fall of 1743. The state of this edition at the time of Pope's death and its disposition thereafter are uncertain, and a paucity of evidence has given rise to some fanciful speculation. In a letter to one of Pope's executors, Bolingbroke suggested that the book be suppressed because lines in "Epistle to a Lady" were thought to satirize the duchess of Marlborough. Since the book lay unpublished until 1748, when it was issued by Warburton with a new title page, Bolingbroke's suggestion is assumed—*post hoc, ergo propter hoc*—to have been adopted.[36] One theory has the executors practicing Mafia-like extortion. In this scenario, Warburton has clear title to the book unless the executors can show that he is violating the terms of the will by publishing "with future alterations." Threatening to expose alleged changes in "Epistle to a Lady," the executors first force the terrorized editor to suppress the book and then, four years later, having achieved their purpose, give him permission to publish the very text on which their earlier threats had been based.[37]

The truth is probably less melodramatic. What must have happened is that the executors interpreted the will's phrase "the property of all . . . my works already printed" to mean copyright only, not copyright and unsold books. In 1751 Warburton reported that "Mr. Pope, at his death, left large impressions of several parts of his Works, unsold; the property of which was adjudged to belong to his executors . . ."—a report confirmed by George Sherburn, who saw letters "which show that about 1748 all the unsold copies of Pope's poems were sold by the executors to Warburton . . ." (*P,* 1:iv).[38] If the phrase "property of all . . . my works" had included unsold books, there would have been nothing for Warburton to buy, since the clause "as he hath written, or shall write commentaries or notes upon" would have given him possession not only of volumes containing his commentary, but of any he might promise to annotate in the future. This open-ended clause, indeed, may be one reason why the executors concluded that copyright was all Pope had intended.[39]

Another reason might have been pressure from the duchess of Marlborough, but if her death in 1744 did not remove all obstacles to release of the book, the publication in 1746 of a folio sheet containing the offending passage should have done so. Why did the edition collect dust for four years? The answer, I believe, is the existence of a legal stalemate: Warburton could not act because the will was interpreted to exclude unsold books from his inheritance; the executors could not act because the death-bed edition contained his commentary, which could not be published without his consent—hence the apparent "suppression" until he bought all the unsold books in 1748.[40]

The seven-year delay in the publication of the *Works* was almost certainly caused in part by legal complexities. But there is no clear evidence of suppression, and no evidence at all of threats based on alleged changes in "Epistle to a Lady."

Faults of the edition. It is no Warburtonian paradox to say that while the edition of Pope has done more than any of his other works to preserve his memory, it has also done more than any other to ruin his reputation. Except for the faithful Hurd, who called it *"the best edition that was ever given of any classic"* (*W,* 1:58), scarcely anyone has had a kind word to say for it. Certainly by the standards of twentieth-century scholarship it is deficient in a number of ways.

Despite the will's prohibition against "future alterations," Warburton tampered with the text. He almost certainly invented the title *Moral Essays* for what Pope called *Epistles,* and he may have invented the title "Prologue to the Satires" for the "Epistle to Dr. Arbuthnot," though here the evidence is ambiguous.[41] He is also probably responsible for turning the "Epistle to Dr. Arbuthnot" and the "Epistle to Bathurst" into dialogues by placing the initial "P." before lines presumably spoken by Pope, and the initials "A." or "B." before lines presumably spoken by Arbuthnot or Bathurst. Since in the "Epistle to Dr. Arbuthnot" Pope himself had placed quotation marks around all but one of the speeches Warburton designates "A.," the change to initials is trifling. In the "Epistle to Bathurst," however, the introduction of dialogue affects the character of the poem, turning the poet's judicious weighing of advantages and disadvantages into a debate between not entirely consistent adversaries.[42] One other important change, in "An Essay on Criticism," is the silent relocation of a couplet to the place it had held before Warburton persuaded Pope to move it.[43]

Another blemish is the gratuitousness of much of the commentary. As one contemporary reviewer complained, "many of the observations and explanations [seem] unnecessary to readers of any tolerable capacity. . . ." One note provides information about Caesar and Cleopatra that must have been known to every eighteenth-century schoolboy, and another identifies Brobdingnag, as if *Gulliver's Travels* were some rare hermetic work instead of one of the most popular and accessible books of the century. Evidently unwilling to withhold from republication anything that he has ever written, Warburton salvages almost all of the *Vindication of the Essay on Man* by dividing it into "Commentary" and "Notes," the former consisting of explication, the latter of attacks on Crousaz. The opening paragraph of the *Vindication* even turns up as a note on the "Epistle to Dr. Arbuthnot."[44]

Occasionally Warburton uses the notes to attack his own enemies. John Gilbert Cooper and Thomas Edwards are pilloried in notes on the "Essay on Criticism," and Edwards reappears as a dunce in a note to the *Dunciad*.[45] A note on line 286 of "Epistle to a Lady" glances satirically at Pope's friend (and possibly mistress) Martha Blount, between whom and Warburton's in-laws there was much bad feeling:

> The Picture of an estimable Woman, with the best kind of contrarieties, created out of the poet's imagination; who therefore feigned those circumstances of a *Husband,* a *Daughter,* and love for a *Sister,* to prevent her being mistaken for any of his acquaintance. And having thus made his *Woman,* he did, as the ancient poets were wont, when they had made their *Muse,* invoke, and address his poem to, her. (*P,* 3:212 n.)

This not only falsely denies that the poem is addressed to Martha Blount but, by declaring that "love for a *Sister*" is a fictional detail, slyly suggests that Martha hated her sister Teresa.

On the other hand, when a passage contains satire on a person or cause that Warburton is sympathetic to, he is reluctant to identify the target. In "The First Epistle of the First Book of Horace," Pope writes ironically that "Our Gen'rals" are not "fond of bleeding, ev'n in *Brunswick's* cause," on which Warburton comments, "In the former Editions it was *Britain's cause.* But the terms are synonymous." Actually Pope never wrote "Britain's cause" and surely never intended that Britain should be thought identical with the house of Brunswick. Though the "Plunging Prelate" of *Dunciad,* book 2, line 323, almost certainly alludes to Warburton's friend and patron Thomas Sherlock, bishop of London, Warburton insists that Pope had emphatically denied the identification. Possibly to please Warburton he had, but an editor less intent on protecting his friends might have been skeptical of the denial. The "Epilogue to the Satires," book 1, line 75, seems to disparage Conyers Middleton's knowledge of Latin. Warburton had resented the slur when the poem first appeared, writing to Middleton that nobody would believe Pope's friend William Murray when he tried to interpret the line as a compliment. In his own note on the line, however, Warburton writes that "what the Poet intended to say, on this occasion, was not to reflect on Dr. Middleton, whom he esteemed and had a personal regard for; but on the contrary, to own the excellence of his judgment. . . ."[46]

From the point of view of later editors and critics, the most problematical aspect of the edition is the changes in the structure of the "Epistle to Cobham" and the "Epistle to Bathurst" that Pope had made at Warburton's suggestion. Warburton begins his commentary on the "Epistle to Cobham" by pointing out that "the order and disposition of the several parts are entirely changed and transposed, tho' with hardly the Alteration of a single Word," the editor having convinced the poet that, "if put into a different form, on an idea he then conceived, [the poem] would have all the clearness of method, and force of connected reasoning." Though it is sometimes conceded that one or two of these alterations are improvements, for the most part they have been condemned even by editors who felt bound to follow them as having Pope's authority (*P*, 3:163).[47] Herbert Davis silently adopts the Warburton text in his Oxford edition,[48] but F. W. Bateson's return in the Twickenham Edition to the original structure of epistles 1 and 3 has reduced Warburton's versions almost to the status of historical curiosities. As far as I know, all scholarly criticism and interpretation of these poems are now based on the Twickenham Edition or on pre-Warburtonian texts.

Warburton's editorial standards. By the standards of twentieth-century scholarship, to repeat, the edition has serious deficiencies. But it is not entirely clear that the standards of twentieth-century scholarship should be applied.

For one thing, Warburton was a literary executor, and "literary executorship," David Nichol Smith points out,

is the very worst preparation for an edition of a great English classic. The problems are entirely different. What is an executor to do with a series of papers that are not quite ready for the press? He is disloyal to the memory of his friend if he perpetuates the little blemishes which his friend would undoubtedly have removed; and if he hits on a happy little alteration which he is convinced his friend would have at once adopted, a rearrangement of words, or the omission of a clumsy or obscure phrase, he may not be the trusty friend that he was expected to be if he stays his hand.[49]

A case in point is Warburton's treatment of variant readings of *An Essay on Criticism*. For an edition of his works in 1736, Pope had asked Jonathan Richardson to transcribe from his manuscript of 1709 deleted lines that would be cited in notes as "Variations." Many such lines Pope did not want transcribed; of those transcribed, some he decided not to print; and of those printed, some he relocated or revised. Clearly he wanted to display his craftsmanship without exposing all the rejects in his cluttered workshop. Warburton continued this policy. Doubtless following the wishes of Pope, who worked with him in preparing the edition with commentary published early in 1744, he printed fewer variations than had appeared in 1736 and a revised version of one that was included for the first time. Robert M. Schmitz, whose excellent edition of the manuscript of 1709 is the source of this information, smiles with a benign tolerance on the omissions and strategic inaccuracies of 1736, characterizing them as "editorial curiosities." Warburton, however, he judges by the most exacting scholarly standards, denouncing him as "unreliable" and "downright perverse."[50] But Warburton's editorial practice is the same as Pope's and is intended to do what Pope expected of a literary executor—to present the poet in the most flattering, not the most revealing, light.

Warburton's treatment of the canon is similarly influenced by the responsibilities of executorship. The editors of the Twickenham Edition *Minor Poems* print every last scrap of verse that can reasonably be attributed to Pope, but Warburton explicitly declares his unwillingness to print anything that would be "unworthy of [Pope's] memory." Thus the Twickenham editors publish 160 miscellaneous poems, Warburton only 53. Though he must have been unaware of many of the Twickenham squibs, he would not have thought their discovery worth the effort of a search and would not have printed most of them even if he could have found them. He is known to have been aware of four poems by Pope that he did not print. Doubtless he was aware of others as well (*P*, 1:lv).[51]

Warburton was not only a literary executor but an eighteenth-century literary executor, which means that his standards of accuracy are not those of the twentieth century. In printing Pope's letters to himself, for example, he silently omits some passages and combines others of different dates.[52] Such practices now seem flagrantly dishonest but were a commonplace in eighteenth-century editions of letters and diaries. "At the risk of being immediately challenged," James Clifford remarks, "I would go so far as to insist that scarcely any volumes of letters or biographical material edited before the twentieth century can be implicitly trusted, either for accuracy of text or for completeness."[53] Some editors went so far as to rewrite the originals, a transgression of which Warburton, at least, is not guilty.

To be sure, standards of accuracy for the texts of poems were more rigorous but still not so rigorous as those of the twentieth century. The silent modernization of typographical conventions is a trivial but suggestive example. John Butt observes that "Since printing house practice was changing at the time [of Warburton's edition], . . . in the use of capital letters and italic type, Warburton's text differs from any text with which Pope was acquainted."[54] In this Warburton was conforming to universal eighteenth-century practice. The modernization of Shakespeare, for example, having begun in the seventeenth century, was continued, silently and as a matter of course, by all eighteenth-century editors. Moreover, there is something to be said for Warburton's modernization of Pope. It represents an extrapolation from a tendency toward typographical simplicity in the taste of the poet as well as of his contemporaries and probably reflects his mature judgment more accurately than do the varied styles of the Twickenham Edition. Warburton's text is at least visually harmonious, while the Twickenham, following the first editions of some of the poems and the last editions of others, is a melange of the elaborate and the austere. Be that as it may, silent modernization in scholarly editions is symptomatic of a more casual attitude toward textual fidelity than twentieth-century readers have come to expect.

In matters of content as well, eighteenth-century editors were less than punctilious—witness the rage for emendation documented in part 1 of this chapter. The later, romantic view of the poem as an expression of the poet's exquisitely sensitive soul encouraged a pious solemnity about the text that in the eighteenth century was reserved for the Scriptures. Warburton, possibly the most reckless practitioner of conjectural emendation in history, treats the text of Job as inviolable. By the twentieth century, emendation of Shakespeare has become virtual sacrilege, but, in the words of one biblical scholar, "there is scarcely a verse in the book [of Job] that has not been subjected to conjectural emendation. . . ."[55] The eighteenth-century attitude toward secular texts was to some extent communicated to editors by the poets themselves, who, craftsmen rather than prophets, were willing to revise for reasons that some later poets would have thought contemptible. Levin L. Schücking calls attention to the profound cultural change represented on the one hand by Pope's eagerness to make revisions suggested by aristocratic friends, and on the other by Shelley's pugnacious opinion that no true artist would revise anything to please anybody.[56] An extreme but significant example is that of James Thomson, who wrote to a friend that he was including in his *Summer* "a Panegyric on Britain, which may perhaps contribute to make my Poem popular."[57] When after Thomson's death his literary executor, Baron Lyttleton, introduced into the text "improvements" that the author had declined to sanction, the editor was perhaps carrying to a logical, if deplorable, conclusion Thomson's own insouciance about the integrity of his poems.[58]

Warburton's unauthorized changes in the text of Pope—the creation of dialogue, for instance, by the addition of initials—must be judged in the light of eighteenth-century attitudes. Bateson calls Warburton "legalistic" for treating the will's prohibitions against "future alterations" as referring only to the words themselves,[59] but from another point of view Bateson's complaint is based on a narrowly legalistic interpretation of Pope's intention. As Warburton understood it, the purpose of Pope's reference to "future alterations" was "to prevent any share of the offense [the poems] might occasion, from falling on the Friend whom he had engaged to give them to the Public" (*P,* 1:iii). It was not intended to keep the editor from editing. Since Pope had every reason to insure that his executor would not feel insulted by the terms of the will, before his death he must have explained the prohibition as Warburton reports it. In any case, considering the number and length of the poems, Warburton's changes are relatively few. In fact, there are probably fewer unauthorized changes in Warburton's text of all of the poems than in the four edited by Bateson, though Warburton's, of course, are silent, Bateson's properly declared.

One other circumstance must be considered if Warburton is to be fairly judged: his collaboration with Pope in revising and annotating the poems. Pope added lines to attack Warburton's enemies and canceled lines to spare his friends. For artistic or theological reasons, he followed Warburton's advice in rewording and reorganizing some of the poems, and he wrote the *Fourth Dunciad*—"the only complete new work in the last five years of his life, and a major achievement of his career"—at Warburton's suggestion and under his influence. To the new four-book *Dunciad* Warburton contributed "Ricardus Aristarchus of the Hero of the Poem" and, alone and in collaboration with Pope, added innumerable satirical notes.[60] Now it is just possible that a twentieth-century editor, given the same relationship with his author (if such a relationship is conceivable in the twentieth century)—it is just possible that a twentieth-century editor might repress his proprietary feelings and treat the text as that of a stranger. But to expect such self-abnegation of an eighteenth-century executor-collaborator seems historically naive. Pope himself tampered with the text of Bolingbroke's *Idea of a Patriot King,* a work he was scarcely authorized to print, much less to edit.[61]

Warburton's role as collaborator is especially relevant to his use of the commentary for his own satirical ends. It is not surprising that when, as he tells Hurd, "a new Dunce or two has come in my way,"[62] he is willing to believe that the poet would have joined him in attacking recently acquired enemies. Besides, though he has been accused of doing so,[63] Warburton never pretends that his "new Dunces" are Pope's. In two notes Cooper and Edwards are clearly cited as the editor's examples, not the poet's, and when Edwards appears as a dunce in a note to the *Dunciad,* the satire depends on the reader's appreciating the editor's cleverness in making the poem apply to someone whom the poet did not have in mind. If the history of the Warburton–Edwards quarrel is known, the joke is apparent; if it is not known, the note is unintelligible and harmless. Even the note denying that the "Epistle to a Lady" is addressed to a real woman lacks satirical bite unless the reader knows that Martha Blount is the "Lady." Warburton must have read the 1745 biography of Pope in which she is so identified. Is his note a serious contradiction of common knowledge or an ironic exploitation of it?[64]

The problem of Warburton's reliability. That Warburton did not feel bound by twentieth-century editorial standards may seem to confirm the worst fears (or fondest hopes) of those who doubt his reliability. But his editorial practice cannot be rationally perceived through a fog of moral outrage. This obscures complexity and leads to the too-easy conclusion that every doubt can be resolved at his ex-

pense. From the point of view of subsequent editors of Pope, Warburton is worse than dishonest. He is unpredictable.

The experience of eighteenth- and nineteenth-century critics and
editors is cautionary. Again and again, on the assumption that Warburton is never to be trusted, conclusions are reached that later evidence shows to be false. Consider, to take a noneditorial example, the
contradiction between Sir Thomas Hanmer's and Warburton's accounts of their collaboration on Shakespeare. Even T. H. Whitaker,
whose review of Hurd's edition of the *Works* is one of the most sympathetic appreciations of Warburton ever written, concludes in the
absence of solid evidence that it must be Hanmer who told the truth.
Unpublished letters now show beyond the shadow of a doubt that
Hanmer lied.[65] Had these not come to light, Warburton's account
would be universally disbelieved and would almost certainly be used
to support further allegations of dishonesty.

More to the point are similar mistakes with regard to the edition
of Pope. Gibbon in the eighteenth century and Courthope in the
nineteenth ridiculed the long note at the end of "The Epilogue to the
Satires," dialogue 1, in which Warburton points out a parallel between Pope's personified Vice and an account by Procopius of the
Empress Theodora. Two passages in Joseph Spence's manuscripts led
James M. Osborn to the discovery that Pope had read a French translation of Procopius, that there are parallels in phraseology between
Pope's lines and the translation, and that Pope had intended a further
allusion to Molly Skerrett, Robert Walpole's second wife. Osborn
concludes that "Warburton's long note was an elaborate irony on the
parallel between the careers of Theodora . . . and Molly Skerrett. . . ."
Courthope expresses a strong suspicion that without Pope's authority
Warburton had removed from the "Epistle to Bathurst" and "The
Epilogue to the Satires," dialogue 1, references to his early patron,
Sir Robert Sutton. Courthope is forced to add a corrective footnote
after reading the manuscript of the letter in which Pope agreed to the
removal of Sutton's name.[66] Had Spence neglected to record the relevant conversations with Pope and Warburton, had the correspondence on Sutton been lost, the note on Theodora and the dropping of
the passages on Sutton would today be cited as evidence of Warburton's unreliability and used to undermine the authority of yet other
passages in the edition of Pope.

Other, similar blunders might be instanced, but a more ambiguous example will illustrate both the dangers of automatic distrust of

Warburton and the complexity of the editorial problem. Courthope discovered a canceled page indicating, he thought, that the title "Prologue to the Satires" for the "Epistle to Dr. Arbuthnot" was Warburton's last-minute invention. In an appendix, he reproduced both the original and the cancel, with the following introductory note:

A COMPARISON of the following cancelled Page of Warburton's edition of 1751 with the equivalent page in the published edition will explain the origin of the second title of the Epistle to Arbuthnot, and of the change of name in the poem now called Epilogue to the Satires. It will be seen that Warburton had written a long and satirical—and it may be added, a very stupid—note upon the couplet found in Pope's MS. after ver. 6 of that Epistle. He seems afterwards to have thought that it might be impolitic to provoke Mallet's resentment, and he accordingly cancelled the page. But as he had to supply the hiatus in the page, left by the removal of the note, he invented the title Prologue to the Satires; and to carry out his idea he called the two Dialogues, published originally under the title of Seventeen Hundred and Thirty-eight, the Epilogue to the Satires. It need hardly be said there is no connection between the Epistle to Arbuthnot and the various Imitations of Horace.[67]

Notice how confidently Courthope declares that Warburton invented the title "Epilogue to the Satires." Given his distrust of Warburton and his certainty that the new title for the "Epistle to Dr. Arbuthnot" is a desperate stop-gap, his conclusion is probably inevitable. It just happens to be false, the title "Epilogue to the Satires" having been invented by Pope in 1740. Courthope's other hypotheses cannot be similarly demolished, but hypotheses they remain. There is no evidence, for instance, that Warburton "thought that it might be impolitic to provoke Mallet's resentment." Indeed, there is just as much evidence for the hypothesis that he canceled the note to make room for the title as for the hypothesis that he invented the title to take the place of the note.[68]

Scholars who want to undermine the authority of a Warburtonian reading invariably cite as evidence other scholars' attacks on the authority of other passages. Fair enough. But perhaps they ought to cite as well, as a warning both to readers and to themselves, the occasions in the past when apparently incontrovertible arguments for Warburton's unreliability have been exploded by the discovery of a single document.

The Editions Compared

The edition of Shakespeare and the edition of Pope bear the marks of the same editorial mind. Both suffer from the editor's arrogance of tone, from his unwillingness to efface himself in favor of his author, and from his itch to regularize, in language or in structure, more than is necessary or desirable in imaginative literature. Though the edition of Pope did not lend itself to conjectural emendation and thus escaped the worst excesses of Warburton's fancy, it lent itself to ingenuity of interpretation. Many impossible emendations in one edition are therefore paralleled by much unconvincing commentary in the other.

Of the two editions, however, the Pope is clearly superior. An unfortunate conjunction of historical circumstances and Warburton's susceptibility to temptation produced in the Shakespeare a monument to the vagaries of the scholarly imagination when it is freed from the constraints of bibliographical knowledge and common sense. That Pope was a contemporary and that his will forbade "future alterations" imposed a discipline that kept the edition of his works within the bounds of sanity. It lacks, to be sure, the punctilious accuracy of twentieth-century scholarship, but it preserves enough of Pope's intention to remain a permanent and indispensable scholarly resource.

Chapter Five
The Letter Writer

Warburton's Styles

Warburton might be said to have two styles, the "polished" and the "unpolished." I use quotation marks to indicate that there is no necessary connection between the elegance of a passage and the amount of labor he might have expended on it. James Crossley says that to his own knowledge there are 20,000 purely stylistic changes in the various editions of the *Divine Legation* alone—all for the worse.[1]

The polished style. The polished style is rare and is characterized by periodic sentences, much parallelism, and, though Warburton's vocabulary is always racy, relatively formal diction. Two good examples are the passage from *Julian* quoted on page 35 above and the following passage from *Remarks on Several Occasional Reflections,* in which a wealth of detail is couched in a variety of parallel constructions to emphasize the absence from the Pentateuch of the doctrine of a future state:

The Bible contains a very circumstantial history of [the Jews] from the time of *Moses* to the great Captivity. Not only of public occurrences, but the private adventures of persons of both sexes, and of all ages and stations, of all characters and complexions; in the lives of virgins, matrons, kings, soldiers, scholars, priests, merchants, husbandmen. They are given too in every circumstance of life, victorious, captive, sick, and in health; in full security and amidst impending dangers; plunged in civil business, or retired and sequestered in the service of religion. Together with their story, we have their compositions likewise. Here they sing their triumphs; there their palinodia: here they offer up their hymns of praise and petitions to the Deity; here they urge their moral precepts to their countrymen; and here again they treasure up their prophecies and predictions for posterity: yet in none of these various casts of composition, do we ever find them acting on the motives, or influenced by the prospect of a *future state;* or indeed expressing the least *hopes* or *fears,* or even common *curiosity* concerning it: but everything they do or say respects the present life only; the good and ill of which are the sole objects of all their pursuits and aversions. (*W,* 11:294–95)

Lucid, forceful, and pleasingly cadenced, its parallelism so varied as
to secure the emphasis of repetition without the sing-song of perfect
balance, this passage is the work of a gifted and self-conscious stylist.
The unpolished style. The unpolished style predominates in
Warburton's work and is accurately described by Samuel Johnson:
"His style is copious without selection, and forcible without neatness;
he took the words that presented themselves: his diction is coarse and
impure, and his sentences are unmeasured."[2] Though one might
quarrel with the implication that the impression of carelessness is always produced by carelessness in fact, Johnson is right about Warburton's diction and the rhythm of his sentences. Examples abound,
but, here, almost at random, is a passage belaboring the hapless John
Tillard, who had had the temerity to challenge Warburton's argument that the ancient philosophers did not believe in a future state
of rewards and punishments:

> I *shall* (says our crafty Advocate [Tillard]) *pass over his nice distinction, di-*
> *visions, and subdivisions.* . . . Now this, I cannot but think hard. He had
> before made his exceptions to *Greek,* and I dare say he would think it unfair
> to have it urged against him after he had so fairly pleaded *Ignoramus* to it;
> yet a critical use of that language is alone sufficient to determine a decisive
> question in this controversy, namely, *of the Spinozism of the ancient philosophers:*
> and here he debars me all benefit of *logic,* and won't have patience while I
> state the question and divide the subject. . . . So that because he knows
> neither *Greek* nor *method,* I shall use none. Here then I might fairly dismiss
> this *minute philosopher,* who dares me to the combat, and yet excepts against
> all the weapons in use. But not to disappoint the company we have brought
> together, I will accept his challenge, and fight him with his own wooden
> dagger. (*W,* 11:154)

Notice the loose, rhythmically irregular third sentence and the
clumsy transformations of "it," first an expletive, then a pronoun
standing for Tillard's ignorance of Greek, then a pronoun standing
for Greek itself. Notice the colloquial "won't" and the racy diction of
the conclusion, which turns theological debate into a brawl. How
much labor Warburton expended on this passage it would be impossible to say. Its effectiveness, though, depends in part on the illusion
of spontaneity, a contemptuous carelessness suggesting that his adversary is not worth the trouble it would take to correct the style.
      Though for many purposes the unpolished style is unsuitable, for
one it is ideal—private communication. It may be for this reason that

Warburton frequently appears to greater advantage in his personal letters than in any other of his writings.

The Letters

Publication and early reception. Of the roughly 1,000 Warburton letters that have survived, about 600 have found their way into print in eighteen scattered sources, where they are inadequately annotated, often carelessly printed, and sometimes expurgated. In Nichols's *Illustrations,* for example, Warburton's report of a promiscuous maid at Cambridge University who "went off the stage, and made her exit with a clap" is emended with ingenious prudery to "made her exit with *eclat.*" His phrase "an arse to wipe" is replaced by asterisks, and "cuckolded" becomes "proved inconstant to." Two carefully obliterated paragraphs in a rare manuscript of a letter printed by Hurd suggest that the Warburton of *Letters from a Late Eminent Prelate* has been similarly bowdlerized.[3]

In spite of timid editing, the merits of the letters were recognized as soon as they began to appear in print in the late eighteenth and early nineteenth centuries. Readers were struck especially by Warburton's power of expression and by his remarkable openness. Edmond Malone, reporting to Bishop Percy that the quarto edition of *Letters from a Late Eminent Prelate* had sold out so quickly that even the queen could not buy a copy, praised the work as "curious and entertaining," but added that it "would certainly have been ten times more so, if several letters had not been suppressed, in which Warburton doubtless conveyed his sentiments in his usual strong and free manner."[4] His strength and freedom of expression were also noticed by William Seward, who called him "one of the best Letter-writers that ever put pen to paper" and declared that his letters "bore great resemblance to his conversation."[5]

Epistolary and conversational styles. The latter observation is confirmed wherever it is possible to compare the record of a conversation with a letter on the same topic, though Warburton probably sounded more jovial in person that he does in print. For example, to Edward Young, author of *Conjectures on Original Composition,* Samuel Richardson wrote, "One of Dr. Warburton's remarks was, that the character of an original writer is not confined to subject, but extends to manner. . . . But he mentioned this with so much good humour, that I should have been glad to have heard you both in

conference upon the subject." Compare Warburton on the same topic
in a letter to Hurd: Young "is the finest writer of nonsense, of any of
this age. And, had he known that *original composition* consisted in the
manner, and not in the matter, he had wrote with common sense,
and perhaps very dully under so insufferable a burthen."[6] Warburton's unwillingness to offend Richardson by denouncing Young explains in part the contrast in tones, but a similar disparity between
the tone of a passage in a letter to Ralph Allen and that of a parallel
anecdote recorded by Joseph Spence suggests that Warburton's epistolary style is that of his conversation minus the good humor. To
Ralph Allen he writes that Dr. James Lesley, a prebendary of Durham, had ordered that a weather vane be fixed in an easterly direction
while he was on a trip to Ireland. Warburton refers contemptuously
to "the spell the blockhead clapt upon the vane" and to "the massi-
ness of his looks and his unconquered taciturnity (for I tried to touch
him to the quick). . . ." Compare Spence's report of Warburton's
conversation: "He's an absolute fo-ol! I saw it the first time I was in
his company, in the horrid massiveness of his look, and that *impene-
trable taciturnity.*"[7] In the opening exclamation and the diphthongi-
zation of "fool," Spence's version suggests not the contempt expressed
in the letter but a drawling delight in Lesley's spectacular stupidity.
It is also noticeable that the diction in Spence is more precise than in
the letter, which means either that Warburton's conversation was
even more pointed than his epistolary prose or, more likely, that he
wrote as he spoke and that Spence edited the style.

In one letter Warburton summarizes a conversation in a way that
almost certainly captures his manner of speaking. In 1772, before
submitting to Parliament a petition for the abolition of the requirement that dissenting ministers subscribe to the Thirty-nine Articles
of the Church of England, three of the leaders called on him to solicit
his support. His account of the meeting is lengthy, but since it has
never been published and is of some importance both as a historical
document and as an illustration of his epistolary and conversational
styles, it is here quoted in full:

The men were [Thomas] Amory, [Richard] Price & one [Andrew] Kippis.—
I received them very Civilly; which it seems, being more than some of the
Bps did, occasioned [(] as you shall find) our parting to be as civil as our
meeting.—When my guests were seated & had told me the occasion of their
visit, I said, that as they professed themselves Christians, & were I believed,

sincerely such, I was a little scandalized at the coldness of their *declaration,* which a Mohametan, or any other Deist was ready to make, & declare with them, that the Scriptures of the old & new Testament contained the will of God, & that they rec^d them for the rule of their Faith & practice. They replied that they made the Declaration in those Terms in order to include as many as they could—But would a Mohametan, said they, receive our Scriptures as the rule of their faith & Practice? I said I did not know but a Mohametan in a qualified sense, might. I was sure, a Deist would. That therefore they should at least have acknowledged the Scriptures to contain the revealed will of God. They thought this but reasonable & as the bill was not yet got through the Commons, they [two illegible words] they were ready to give this Satisfaction—I afterwards found that they did so—I told them that when I mentioned Mohametans & Deists, it was only to show in what these petitioners were wanting, & not to give my opinion of the right that Mohametans & Deists had to a toleration.—And so far I would say too, that if I found these two Sects in possession of a toleration, I should not be amongst the first to attempt to deprive them of it.—They had now for the best part of an age neglected, with impunity to qualify themselves as the Law directs. If ever I found them punished for this, I promised them to vote in their defence—*In the meantime,* they must excuse me for voting with my Brethren ag^t this Bill.—After a long, & no disagreeable conversation with them, concerning the nature & intent of religious toleration, we parted, & at going away Amory (who we may call, the *Dean of the corporation*) very politely assured me he would make it his business to do me the justice to assure all his friends that I was perfectly consistent in my notions & actings, on this occasion—From whence I collected that I had been represented otherwise.

That Warburton's version of the encounter conveys the spirit if not the letter of his conversation is independently confirmed by one of the participants. "The only time I had ever the honour of being in his company," Andrew Kippis writes, "which was an hour and a half in his study, I found him condescending in his manner, and admirably instructive in his conversation."[8]

Rarity of concrete detail and personal confession. One notices in the passage on visiting dissenters how skillfully a conversation lasting over an hour has been reduced to essentials. One also notices a paucity of physical detail. Like most letter writers of the eighteenth century, Warburton almost never gives information about the particularities of everyday life—about what people eat, drink, wear, or look like; about how they spend the day; about the look of the countryside or of city streets or of the rooms that life is lived in. Concrete detail

appears almost exclusively as metaphor and is used not for its own
sake but for the sake of the abstract idea that the metaphor is intended to clarify. When literal detail does appear, it is startling for
its rarity. Warburton tells Robert Taylor, for instance, that a piece
he had published in a newspaper was written "by your Kitchen Fire
on your Wedding Day, partly before my going to Winthorpe [to of-
ficiate at the wedding], partly after. But I would not trouble you
with a foolish Quarrel on a Day devoted to Joy." This brief passage
grips the imagination in a way that entire letters, for all of their other
merits, do not. One thinks of the excited preparations before the
wedding and the noisy celebration afterward, while Warburton writes
alone by the kitchen fire. Another vivid picture appears in the account of the prosecution of John Wilkes in Parliament. At the conclusion of an angry speech, Warburton reports, William Pitt "thrust
out his crutch in the action of a man driving a noxious animal from
him."[9]

Almost equally rare is personal confession. Of course the letters
contain many expressions of feeling, but the language is usually conventional and hides as much as it reveals. Even the death of Warburton's son, a loss from which he never recovered, calls forth in a letter
to Thomas Balguy only the predictable formulas of grief and resig-
nation. Occasionally, however, a passage is so strikingly personal in
tone as to suggest unreserved candor. Here is a reply to a complaint
from Balguy that Warburton has not answered his last letter:

I did not think that any of your letters would ever give me pain. But this
did a great deal. Tho' I deserved it—not for my neglect or forgetfulness,
but for the innate folly of my procrastinating temper. I had it a hundred
times in my thoughts to make my acknowledgements for your favour of last
November, & I abused the liberty of a friend by deferring it from day to
day.[10]

The unaffected graciousness of this apology depends in part on the
implied compliments (he can be hurt by Balguy's displeasure; Balguy
has been "a hundred times" in his thoughts); and in part on the apparent artlessness of the style ("But this did a great deal. Tho' I deserved it"). Indeed, perhaps owing to feelings of guilt, Warburton
often writes with special poignance whenever his own indolence and
procrastination are the subject. He tells Taylor that "writing even at
leisure you know is most irksome to me," and in an extraordinary
letter to Philip Doddridge he confesses that he is so constitutionally

lazy and so bored by the subject of the *Divine Legation* that he has had to force himself to finish the second volume by telling his printer to start the presses running. Nor is indolence, he continues, his only fault:

Distractions of various kinds, inseparable from human life, joined with a naturally melancholy habit, contribute greatly to increase my indolence, and force me often to seek in letters nothing but mere amusement. This makes my reading wild and desultory: and I seek refuge from the uneasiness of thought from any book, let it be what it will, that can engage my attention. . . . By my manner of writing upon subjects, you would naturally imagine, they afford me pleasure, and attach me thoroughly. I will assure you, No. I have amused myself much in human learning, to wear away the tedious hours inseparable from a melancholy habit.[11]

Warburton may exaggerate his melancholy, but the self-portrait is convincing because it does not seem intended to increase Doddridge's admiration for his work. Discussing the passage with William Hazlitt, James Northcote favorably contrasted the evident sincerity of Warburton's self-deprecation with "the common coquetry both of authors and artists, to be supposed to do what excites the admiration of others with the greatest ease. . . ."[12]

Sentiments of men and things. "I spoke my sentiments freely of men and things, because this is my way," Warburton writes of his letters to Conyers Middleton; "therefore it cannot but be that there must be things in them which will give offense."[13] He might have said the same of all his letters, for it is freedom in the expression of opinion that constitutes the openness his contemporaries admired. Almost every letter longer than a note contains general observations— on literature, on politics, on the church, on individuals. Though these observations are sometimes expressed with a judicious seriousness, the tone is more often comic or extravagantly contemptuous. William Mason, noticing the frequency of the word "scoundrel" in Warburton's letters, remarks, "It was rather a *Cant* word with the good Bishop, than any mark of violent resentment."[14] Like "villain," "wretch," and "blockhead," which occur as often, "scoundrel" is hyperbolical, an exaggerated gesture in a satirical performance. Warburton knows that his friends know that he is theatrically outrageous, and at times he is probably driven to satirical extremes by the belief that some new extravagance is expected of him in every letter.

Though he never achieves the subtle ironies of a Swift or a Fielding, he can almost match his great contemporaries in the use of some of the other techniques of satire. For instance:

Mock epic. At a local dinner party, he tells Taylor, one of the guests, a lover of pudding, was

tempted by the richest side of a very inviting one when lo! as he sprung forward to the Engagement the Pudding—

> *fled before him.*
> *The Floor gave way. The solemn crack dismays*
> *The sinking hearts of men. Where should they turn*
> *Distress'd? Whence seek for aid? When from below*
> *Hell threatens, & ev'n Fate unseen gave signs*
> *Of Wrath & Desolation. Vain were Vows*
> *Or Execrations dire.—The Pudding still*
> *Ralph undismay'd pursues. Alas! in vain.*
> *It with it's Votries in one Ruin shared*
> *Crush'd & oerwhelm'd.—*

In plain *English* the Floor continued to sink evenly & gently downwards till it came to the Barrels in the Cellar, but then that side tipped the Floor all awry like a Ship that stumbles on a Quicksand & in a most pitiful manner run the good Company & the good chear together.

Epigrammatic phrasing. Of "Dr." John Hill: "his Belly . . . is the primum mobile of all his actions. He would write ag' me for one dinner, & write in my favour for two." Of a tyrannical patron: "The doting old man gives you roast meat & would beat you with the spit." The bishop of Gloucester to a Methodist-leaning clergyman in his diocese: "I shall insist upon your constant residence in your parish, not so much from the good you are likely to do there, as to prevent the mischief you may do by rambling about in other places."

Animal and insect imagery. Of Horace Walpole: "The man seems to be produced in the order of things just as a worm is in a flourishing Cedar, to stop its growth & poison its juices." Of the neglect of the Reverend John Towne by the first family of his parish: "during 30 years, all which time he has been under their nose they have never had the sagacity of one of their Hounds, to make a right point, or instinct enough to snuff up superior merit in the air; but have lived & rioted on Carrion. . . ."

Puns. Reporting what he had replied to Bolingbroke when asked if the clergy still smoked as much as ever: "The Orthodox Clergy still smoaked [sic], but the Heretical *took snuff*. But tho this was the distinguishing badge of either party yet it seemed after all, to be an adherence & agreement to the same thing only taken in a different way." Of the decline of literature:

I take quibling [sic] to be as certain a sign of expiring Sense as rattling in the Throat is of expiring Life. Yet in an Epitaph on a Woman dying in Child-Birth I was scandalized to see the two following Lines so unbecoming the Gravity of the Author & the Dignity of the Occasion.

> *And finding none to take her PART*
> *Labour & pains soon broke her Heart.*

(Was there really such an epitaph? Was he really scandalized?)

Name-calling. Lamenting that the Reverend Edmund Law should have had the good fortune to marry an attractive and sensible woman: "She has a good person, of so amiable & gentle manners, so humble in her demeanor, & so reasonable in her sentiments, that it provoked me to think, that she, who would have made the happiness of a Man, was fallen to the lot of this Quiddity, this Remnant of a School-subtilty."

Scatological imagery. Of a friend who, after dabbling in the liberal arts, devotes himself to the study of ancient medals: "You must have seen in Summer time a large black Flesh-Fly, full of *Embrio* maggots[,] with a Spirit of Liberty & appearance of Taste[,] take a Tour of a delicious Garden, where Sweets of the *Heliotrope,* the *Tulip* & the *Polyanthes* do each in their turn engage the sprightly Creature's Curiosity till at length he settles as in his native Habitation & takes a hearty Repast on a Turd." Of radical Whig politics: "I can hardly bear the Word Liberty, when it becomes of that Species for which the Corsicans of old, of whom the Greek proverb: 'The Corsicans are free, they may *shit* where they please.' So are the English. And glorying in this Freedom, Tom Wharton the Marquis in a late Reign did it on the Altar & now, the execrable Wilkes has done it on the throne."[15]

Sense and sensibility. When he is not being satirical, Warburton occasionally descends to the sentimentality and boastful moralizing that some eighteenth-century letter writers and readers seem to favor. John Nichols, for example, calls "admirable" Warburton's letter to William Stukeley upon the death of his first wife:

> I never thought a Letter from you could have given me the concern I feel at the melancholy contents of yours. This loss has revived in me all that tenderness I so lately felt for a very deserving Sister—and the tears I am now shedding, which have a little interrupted me, is an equal tribute to the memory of two good women.
>
> You know I have not the best opinion of the sex, which always made my esteem for a woman of worth, where she was found, proportionably greater than that the generality of men have. And it is now with the greatest concern I say it, as I have frequently before done it with the greatest pleasure, that Mrs. Stukeley, for all those good qualities that make a woman of sense admired, was the first in my esteem. In a word, I am wrung with the sincerest grief you can imagine. . . .[16]

And so on. The pause for weeping seems excessive, and the passage on his uncommon esteem for worthy women seems as much intended to parade his own sensitivity and virtue as to console Stukeley. But such passages of sentimentality and indirect self-praise are fortunately rare and, like the recent practice of demonstrating one's sincerity by making embarrassing personal revelations, may be attributed to fashion rather than to some singular lapse of taste.

Warburton is at his most impressive when he has a clearly defined practical purpose: to convey information, to make a request, to give a command, to persuade to action. Though utility does not always exclude wit (see the letter to the Reverend John Andrews quoted on p. 96 above), the practical letters are notable for other virtues: clarity, quiet authority, and naturalness of expression. "In speaking of Warburton's intellect," James Boaden remarks of a letter to David Garrick describing an estate the latter considered buying, "it should be observed that he can do even slight things with unexpected ease and gracefulness. Who ever described 'a patch of land' better, than it is done in the present letter?"[17]

To illustrate Warburton's expository and persuasive eloquence, here in full is a hitherto unpublished letter to Sir Thomas Hanmer, a letter of biographical as well as stylistic importance. Following the rupture in their friendship, Hanmer declared that Warburton had initiated the relationship between them and had visited Mildenhall, Hanmer's residence, uninvited. This version of events was generally credited until challenged by A. W. Evans on the evidence of Hanmer's unpublished letters.[18] The present letter, unknown to Evans, confirms the truth of his argument.

Newarke May 21 1739

Sir,

Having been informed that you was in treaty with a Bookseller about a new Edition of Shakespear, I beg leave to remind you of all that has pass'd between us: not with any intention to complain; for that is below me; but in order to shew the justice of the request I am going to make to you; and which occasions you this trouble.

About three Years ago my Lord of Salisbury [Bishop Thomas Sherlock], whose favours to me necessarily give him an absolute power over me, desired I would communicate to you what remarks I had made upon Shakespear: which command I so readily complied with, that I immediately put into your hands a paper I chanced to have then in Town; and, as soon as I got down into the Country, began a weekly correspondence on my part, which continued for about a twelvemonth: In which I transcribed a great number of notes, remarks, & emendations &c. sufficient to furnish out a new Edition. And all this without the least reserve.

When this was done, you was pleased to invite me, the following Summer, to Mildenhall, to look over your book. I went. I looked it over: and, before I left you, made you the offer of taking upon my selfe the drudgery of a new Edition, where the text should be settled according to your own pleasure. You appeared not to be averse to it: but gave me to understand, that as you intended no profit to your selfe from the Edition, so I was not to look for any. I took the liberty of telling you that such intention became your quality: but that conduct which was sutable [*sic*] to your fortune & Station would be a ridiculous affectation in mine. There the matter rested till my return; and then I repeated, in a letter to you, the substance of my offer; and endeavoured to shew the reasonableness of it. To this you returned me for answer, that you believed it could not be made worth my while to undertake a new edition. Notwithstanding all this discouragement, amidst all my endeavours to oblige you, I still, Sir, you know, went on in communicating to you, with my usual frankness, my Observations on Shakespear, and in returning the best answers I could to your Queries.

Last Spring you was pleased to informe me you should be in London ab[t] Easter, & expressed an inclination of seeing me there. I wrote you word I should be there. I was so & paid my respects to you. I then expected you had considered fully of the matter, & would communicate your thoughts freely to me. To engage you to declare your selfe I told you, as was true, that I had been asked by some of the Society for the Encouragement of learning to print an Edition of Shakespear with them. And, at the same time to assure you that I was disposed to do nothing but in concert with you, I told you, you might expect to be troubled with some more of my remarks on Shakespear. Yet all this drew nothing from you. And you forced me to leave you in an Opinion that you resolved I should have no concern in the Edition. And now it appears I was not mistaken. After all this I thought my selfe at liberty to declare publicly that I would give an Edition of Shakespear my selfe. Which was only returning to the resolution in which my Lord Bishop of Sarum found me when he first asked me to communicate my remarks to you. And to shew the Public I am in earnest, I have given a specimen & Plan of a New Edition to the Authors of the Universal Dictionary to be inserted into the Article of Shakespear.

This, Sir, I am sure you will do me the Justice to own is a true State of the Case. You hold your selfe disengaged I complain not. All I mean is to shew the reasonableness of my request. Which is only this—that you would be so good as to return me all my letters of remarks & papers; and, as the contents of them are as much my property as any thing can be any Man's, that you would be pleased to dispense with doing me the Honour of using or inserting any of the emendations or Remarks into your Edition. A place where I should have the greatest honour to appear in, but that I shall, my selfe, have occasion for those materials. This request is perhaps in part needless. For I remember you told me you intended to have no notes, but that your emendations should support themselves. But as the complying with it is a matter of great Consequence to me tho' of little or none to you, you will be so good to excuse my having made it, & for now again repeating it. Be pleased to send the letters & papers sealed up, to Mr Gyles's Bookseller in Holborne who will convey them to me. Your Compliance with this will engage me to profess my selfe

> Hon^d Sr Your most [tear in MS]
> humble Servant
> W. Warburton[19]

When word of Samuel Johnson's famous letter to Lord Chesterfield reached Warburton, he asked the Reverend William Adams "to carry his compliments to [Johnson], and to tell him, that he honoured him for his manly behaviour in rejecting these condescensions of Lord Chesterfield, and for resenting the treatment he had received from him, with a proper spirit."[20] Possibly Warburton was reminded of his letter to Hanmer, in its own way intended to reproach an irresponsible social superior. Warburton's lacks the brilliance of Johnson's, the magnificent irony that universalizes a minor literary quarrel. But in justice to Warburton, it must be remembered that his situation was different from Johnson's. He could not risk offending Hanmer, who had control of his papers, or Bishop Sherlock, who had the power to block his advancement in the church. (The detailed summary of his relationship with Hanmer is partly intended for Sherlock, to whom he sent a draft of the letter.)[21] Given the delicacy of his task, his tone seems exactly right—courteous and dignified but not without traces of sarcasm. Nowhere in any of his works does he appear to better advantage than when he reiterates his refusal to ape Hanmer's patrician disdain for money.

Johnson's letter to Chesterfield strengthened his title to literary immortality. Warburton's achievement was less august but more immediate: Hanmer returned the papers.[22]

The Man in the Letters

Johnson rightly ridicules the belief that personal letters bare the soul,[23] but it is hard to resist the impression that one knows intimately the writer of almost a thousand letters written to a variety of correspondents over a period of fifty years. A man's character may be the sum of his favorite poses, and these, at least, his letters will reveal.

The man one seems to get to know in Warburton's letters is far from uniformly attractive. He has a nasty habit, for example, of ridiculing his friends behind their backs.[24] For this, however, he has indirectly supplied his own defense. "One may as well expect to be warmed by moonshine," he writes Balguy concerning patrons, "as by the influence of some of our Chaster luminaries. I like a genial orb that will warm tho' it may burn."[25] He was a genial orb, and those closest to him were always in danger of being singed by the heat of his satire.

But admitting this fault and others—a too great readiness to feel contempt; a fondness for dogmatic and unoriginal generalizations, especially concerning politics; an inability to recognize his own intellectual limitations—admitting all this, the Warburton of the letters is nonetheless a man it is possible to like and admire. He can be playful, warm, generous, and kind. This needs to be emphasized because his current reputation as an unpleasant bully, derived solely (and selectively) from his public writings, conflicts with what is known about the affection he inspired in his friends. The following anecdote is instructive. In 1765, his publishers, Jacob Tonson and Andrew Millar, asked Samuel Johnson to soften his criticism of Warburton in

his soon-to-be-published edition of Shakespeare. Tonson and Millar
can have had no financial motive in making this request, since Warburton's Shakespeare was an obvious commercial failure and no longer
in print. Nor is it likely that Johnson, who, without removing all of
his strictures, went to the trouble of canceling sixteen pages, would
have cut his opinions to line somebody's pockets. He must have been
asked to spare the old man's feelings. Warburton's letters give
glimpses of the friend whom Tonson and Millar wanted to protect.[26]

Chapter Six
Conclusion

Warburton's Reputation

The history of Warburton's reputation deserves a doctoral dissertation, not because the subject is intrinsically important, but because it is potentially fruitful of knowledge about the psychology of literary opinion. The following impressionistic sketch is intended only to account for his humble place in the ranks of minor English writers.

Warburton in the nineteenth century. In spite of suggestions in the last decades of the eighteenth century that his most famous work was already being forgotten,[1] there is evidence that he continued to hold his own for another fifty or sixty years. Editions of his collected works appeared in 1811 and 1841, of the *Alliance between Church and State* in 1848, and of the *Divine Legation* in 1837 and 1846. There were three English editions of the letters to Hurd (1808–9) and two American editions (both 1809 and both claiming to be the first in America). Kilvert's *Selections from the Unpublished Papers* appeared in 1841. Perhaps more suggestive of his prestige than republication or the lavish praise of critics like James Crossley and T. D. Whitaker are incidental allusions assuming the general reader's familiarity with his works. A sermon published by the president of Bowdoin College in 1815, for example, quotes respectfully from the *Divine Legation* in a footnote, identifying the source only with the words, "says Warburton." In a theological work published in 1836, the author warns that some readers will fail to understand his chapter on Warburton because they will ignore what precedes it in their haste to read about him.[2]

A precipitous decline in his reputation—a fall from which it has never recovered—occurred after 1850. J. Selby Watson's lengthy biography was published in 1863, but Watson's indifference to his subject infects almost everything in the book except Warburton's anti-Methodism, of which the author happens to approve. After 1848 Warburton's works were no longer reprinted, and by 1879 a rare admirer could begin an appreciation of the *Divine Legation* by calling it "nearly forgotten."[3] Mark Pattison's generally favorable review of Watson's *Life* combines tepid praise of Warburton with icy denunciation and must have been all the more damaging for its apparent fair-mindedness. Leslie Stephens's furious chapter on Warburton in *The History of English Thought in the Eighteenth Century* is every freethinker's revenge for the savaging of the fraternity in the *Divine Legation*.[4]

A simultaneous decline in the reputation of Samuel Johnson[5] suggests that Warburton was as much the victim of new cultural attitudes as of his own very real deficiencies. To satisfy Pattison, for example, the *Divine Legation* would have had to be not just a better book but a different book altogether, for he defines theology in such a way as to rule Warburton's methodology out of court. Pattison's true theologian communes with heaven rather as a Wordsworthian communes with nature, theology being "the contemplative, speculative habit, by means of which the mind places itself already in another world than this. . . ." Attempts to prove that this can be done merely insure that it will not be done, and "When an age is found occupied in proving its creed, this is but a token that the age has ceased to have a proper belief in it." Naturally the ascension of the mind to another world requires the proper solemnities—hence Pattison's complaint that Warburton lacks "religious earnestness" and "personal religion," the want of which accounts for "the secular and official tone" that Pattison finds in most eighteenth-century religious discourse.[6] Warburton is condemned in part for not thinking like a Victorian and in part for not sounding like one.

No doubt many other circumstances combine to produce the change in his reputation: an understandable and justified reaction to the excessive praise heaped on him by earlier admirers; the general public's growing indifference to theology of any kind; and a new conception of the creative imagination that confers higher status on any routine poem, play, or novel than on all but the most brilliant works of nonfictional prose. One additional circumstance is especially important, however, because it still obtains in the twentieth century: Warburton's association with Pope.

Warburton and the Popeans. In his study of Pope's eighteenth-century reputation, W. L. MacDonald declares that Warburton was "little short of a disaster for Pope's memory." Owing to the commentator's truculence, "the poet's worst qualities have been kept in the foreground during almost two centuries of criticism." A recent reference work says that Warburton's "clumsy editing and insensitive 'improvements' . . . did something to blight Pope's reputation." None of this will bear scrutiny. MacDonald almost immediately contradicts himself by asserting that "In the nineteenth century much of the hostility to Pope was transferred in [*sic*] his clerical commentator, and 'hunting out' Warburton became a critical pastime. . . ." A few chapters later he pushes this phenomenon back to the late eighteenth century, remarking of Joseph Warton's edition of Pope that "Warburton was already functioning as the lightning rod that diverted the thunderbolts of abuse from Pope to himself."[7] But if the lightning-rod effect existed at all, MacDonald might have found it operating as early as 1751. Published in that year, *Verses Occasioned by Mr. Warburton's Late Edition of Mr. Pope's Works* expressed nothing but sympathy for the poet while comparing Warburton's notes to obscene graffiti on the "sacred walls" of St. Paul's cathedral, to out-houses on the banks of "Thames' silver flood," and so on.[8] It might even be said that Pope's reputation was enhanced by the encomiastic metaphors the anonymous satirists had to invent for the poetry to emphasize by contrast the desecratory nature of the annotation.

Actually there is no more evidence that Warburton deflected the lightning than that he caused it. Pope's reputation is one thing, Warburton's another. To be sure, critics who were hostile to Pope were also hostile to Warburton and might use him as a stick to beat the poet with, but he was never the only stick or even the biggest one. On the other hand, admirers of Pope were, if anything, even more hostile to Warburton than Pope's enemies. While reviewers of the Elwin–Courthope edition of Pope complained of Elwin's hostility to the poet, none to my knowledge complained of hostility to the commentator.[9] Thus developed, at a time when Warburton's reputation was plunging for a variety of other reasons, a *de facto* alliance between Popeans and anti-Popeans that has lasted for more than a hundred years. "To all Pope's admirers," one scholar has recently declared, "the name of Warburton is anathema."[10] This too-sweeping generalization is in one respect not sweeping enough. The name of Warburton is anathema to Pope's detractors as well.

Warburton in the twentieth century. All this is not to say that Warburton would now be heading the best-seller lists if it were not for Pope. Partisans of Theobald, Bolingbroke, and Hume have their own reasons for joining the anti-Warburton alliance. Moreover, since anyone who has heard of Warburton at all is more likely to have heard of him as the editor of Pope than in any other connection, his memory steals much of its pale fire from the poet's. But if that dazzling star is temporarily obscured, Warburton can be seen to burn with a dim light of his own. Theobald partisans aside, twentieth-century Shakespeare scholars display little hostility to Warburton, treating him at worst as a harmless eccentric. Unlike the much superior edition of Pope, which arouses animosity because the authority of its readings must be destroyed before they are rejected, the edition of Shakespeare can be consulted for what it has to offer and then guiltlessly ignored. As for the theology, students of church history recognize in *The Alliance between Church and State* an original and thought-provoking theory of establishment.[11] To my knowledge no one in this century has taken seriously the central thesis of the *Divine Legation,* but critics have found much to respect in individual chapters. The ingenious interpretation of Egyptian hieroglyphics has a permanent place in the history of decipherment,[12] and the discovery of parallels between the initiation ceremony of the Eleusinian Mysteries and Aeneas's descent to the underworld will have to be taken into account as long as Virgil's epic continues to be read. Respect for Warburton's criticism might be further increased if future anthologists of eighteenth-century literature would print one of the shorter interpretive essays—that on *The Golden Ass,* say, or on Hamlet's attitude toward Aeneas's tale to Dido—familiarity with which would make less inexplicable Pope's opinion that he was "the greatest general critic I ever knew." A judicious, well-edited selection of the letters would also reveal that he was not the ogre that his brutal manners in controversy make him seem, and would help to resolve an obvious but seldom-acknowledged paradox: that the much-admired satires of the poet who made the ogre his friend are based in part on a shrewd understanding of the characters of men.

A Final Judgment

Warburton's worst fault as a writer is his inability to distinguish between the sensible and the foolish. By a kind of self-hypnosis, he convinces himself of the truth of an absurdity—a theological paradox, a literary interpretation, a textual emendation—and then lavishes upon it powers of logic and invention that deserve the most lofty purposes. When a higher purpose does present itself—and such occasions are more frequent than is generally recognized—he can be astute, original, and solid. It is understandable that he has often been held in contempt for abusing gifts of intellect and imagination that sounder thinkers must envy. But perhaps he should be pitied for lacking the good judgment that would have made him a major theologian, scholar, and critic.

Notes and References

Preface

1. Cf. W. Ray Rhine, "Relation of Birth Order, Social Class, and Need Achievement to Independent Judgment," *Journal of Social Psychology* 92 (1974):206—"Birth order is an ecological variable that summarizes imprecisely a large number of empirical differences between first- and later borns. . . ." Writing ten years earlier, William D. Altus, "Birth Order and its Sequelae," *Science* 151 (1964):44–49, surveyed the history of birth-order studies and found no evidence to contradict the hypothesis that first-born and only children are more likely to be eminent than middle or youngest children.

2. John Norman Pearson, *A Critical Essay on the Ninth Book of Bishop Warburton's "Divine Legation of Moses"* (Cambridge, 1808).

3. Except for Warburton's dates, which are known from other sources, the dates of birth and death must be approximated, since the parish registers list dates of baptism and burial only. Technically Warburton is not a first-born child. A sister, Elizabeth, was baptized on 6 November 1697 and buried three days later. The other children's dates of baptism are as follows: Mary, 12 July 1700; Elizabeth, 22 September 1702 (naming a child after a dead sibling was not uncommon); Frances, 11 November 1704; George, 5 July 1706. A George, "son of Mrs. Warberton [*sic*], widow," was buried on 23 August 1709. Mr. Cook suspects that this is a different George, but Warburton's only brother is known to have died in childhood, and it seems unlikely that in the same town there would be two Warburton widows, each with a son George who died young. For William's dates and the burial date of his mother, see the chronology.

Chapter One

1. C. R. [James Crossley], "The Literary Character of Bishop Warburton and Dr. Johnson," *Blackwood's* 8 (1820):243; Joseph Stratford, *Gloucestershire Biographical Notes* (Gloucester, 1887), p. 112.

2. Warburton's plagiarism—from Milton's *Areopagitica*—appears in his *Enquiry into the Causes of Prodigies and Miracles* (London, 1727), pp. 136–37. On Warburton's linguistic errors, see John Upton, *Critical Observations on Shakespeare,* 2d ed. (1748; reprint ed., New York: AMS Press, 1973), pp. xii–xvi, li; and J. Selby Watson, *The Life of Warburton* (London, 1863), pp. 128–30. On the argument of the *Divine Legation of Moses demonstrated,* 2 vols. (London, 1738–41), see p. 26. On Warburton's private character, see p. 3.

3. Warburton to Hurd, [December 1755], in *Letters From a Late Eminent Prelate*, 2d ed. (London, 1809), p. 203. For more details on Warburton's letters, see Chapter 5.

4. *The Works of the Right Reverend William Warburton*, 12 vols. (London, 1811), 1:116–17; hereafter cited in the text as *W*.

5. Ibid., p. 3.

6. A. W. Evans, *Warburton and the Warburtonians* (London, 1932), p. 132; Benjamin Boyce, *The Benevolent Man* (Cambridge, Mass, 1967), pp. 223, 232.

7. Lawrence Stone, *The Family, Sex and Marriage in England: 1500–1800* (New York: Harper, 1977), pp. 405, 413.

8. See Preface, n. 3.

9. 9 March 1737/8, British Library add. MSS 32,458, f. 37.

10. Warburton to Stukeley, 24 December 1737, in William Dickinson, *The History and Antiquities of the Town of Newark* (Newark, 1816), pp. 202–4.

11. Notebook 1, letters 3–4, 6, 10, 13: the notebooks—which contain manuscript copies of Warburton's letters—are at the Harry Ransom Center, University of Texas, Austin. Cf. Ross Stagner, *Psychology of Personality*, 3d ed. (New York: McGraw-Hill, 1965), p. 421: "First-born boys who have a sib two to four years younger are rated very high on hostility, jealousy, and other anger-related traits; whereas boys whose sib is less than two years or more than four years younger do not rate nearly so high on these attributes."

12. Evans, *Warburton*, pp. 202–3, 272–7. Initiating a correspondence with Warburton after having met him for the first time, Charles Yorke wrote, "I own, what I then saw of you made me consider you in a different light from what I had done [on the basis of Warburton's books], but in a light no less striking and more amiable" (British Library add. MSS 35,404, f. 1). A reviewer in *The History of the Works of the Learned*, n.s. 1 (1742):415, applied to him the line "The best good Man with the worst-natured Muse."

13. Ezra Stotland et al., *Empathy and Birth Order: Some Experimental Explorations* (Lincoln: University of Nebraska Press, 1971), p. 49. For somewhat different but very plausible hypotheses about role-learning within the family constellation, see Orville B. Brim, Jr., "Personality Development as Role-Learning," in *Personality Development in Children*, ed. Ira Iscoe and Harold W. Stevenson (Austin: University of Texas Press, 1960), pp. 148–49.

14. Stone, *The Family, Sex and Marriage in England*, p. 448. Stone also reports (p. 115) the experience of an eight-year-old boy who, when sent away to school, "missed his sister so much that he ran away from school and made the long and lonely walk home in order to be with her." An additional source of anxiety for Warburton at this time may have been the presence of a rival male sibling. See Preface, n. 3.

15. Watson, *Life*, p. 3.

16. Evans, *Warburton,* pp. 125–26, 133–34; William Merritt Sale, Jr., *Samuel Richardson: A Bibliographical Record of His Literary Career with Historical Notes* (1936; reprint ed., Hamden, Conn.: Archon Books, 1969), p. 61.

17. Warburton to Lowth, 12 October 1756, in *Works,* 12:463.

18. Stotland, *Empathy and Birth Order,* pp. 50–51, reports that first-born children may be both parentlike and childlike.

19. John Nichols, *Literary Anecdotes of the Eighteenth Century,* 9 vols. (London, 1812–16), 5:536.

20. *The Family Memoirs of William Stukeley . . . ,* 3 vols., Publications of the Surtees Society, vols. 73, 76, 80 (Durham, England: Andrews & Co. for the Society, 1882–87), 1:129.

21. Relations between Theobald and Warburton can be followed in their surviving correspondence in Nichols, *Illustrations of the Literary History of the Eighteenth Century,* 8 vols. (London, 1817–58), 2:204–654, and in Richard Foster Jones, *Lewis Theobald* (New York, 1966), pp. 265–345. The three attacks on Pope appeared in the *Daily Journal* for 22 March, 8 April, and 22 April 1729, and, on the basis of circumstantial evidence, were first attributed to Warburton by T. R. Lounsbury, *The Text of Shakespeare: Its History from the Publication of the Quartos and Folios down to and Including the Publication of the Editions of Pope and Theobald* (New York: Scribner's, 1906), pp. 346–62. Further evidence of Warburton's authorship is contained in my article "Warburton's Copy of Theobald's *Shakespeare,*" *Transactions of the Cambridge Bibliographical Society* 7 (1980):451.

22. Evans, *Warburton,* pp. 196–97. Middleton's letter was published by Warburton's protégé John Towne in *The Argument of the Divine Legation Fairly Stated* (London, 1751), pp. 162–72, and introduced as "an ingenious and acute Objection against the Argument of the *Div. Leg.* urged in a very learned and masterly manner. . . ."

23. Evans, *Warburton,* p. 236.

24. The review of Crousaz's *Examen de l'Essai de M. Pope sur l'Homme* and *Commentaire sur la Traduction en verse de M. l'Abbé du Resnel de l'Essai de Mr. Pope sur l'Homme* is in *Bibliothèque Raisonnée* 21 (1738):215–27. Warburton's letters are in the *General Evening Post,* 12–14 December 1738, p. 1, and *The History of the Works of the Learned,* December 1738, pp. 425–66; January, February, March, May 1739, pp. 56–73, 89–105, 159–72, 330–58. The latter five letters, with the addition of a sixth, were published as *A Vindication of Mr. Pope's Essay on Man* (London, 1740). *A Critical and Philosophical Commentary on Mr. Pope's Essay on Man* (London, 1742) conflates into four the six letters of the *Vindication* and a separately published *Seventh Letter* (London, 1740). For Pope's first letter to Warburton, see *The Correspondence of Alexander Pope,* ed. George Sherburn, 5 vols. (Oxford: Clarendon Press, 1956), 4:163–64.

25. To my knowledge, the earliest allegation of Warburton's initially

unfavorable opinion of the *Essay on Man* is by Zachary Grey, *A Word or Two of Advice to William Warburton* (London, 1746), p. 2.

26. Stukeley, *Family Memoirs* (Durham, 1882) 1:127–28.

27. Samuel Johnson, *Lives of the English Poets,* ed. George Birkbeck Hill, 3 vols. (1905; reprint ed., New York: Octagon, 1967), 3:169. Cf. Warburton to Murray, 2 July 1738, in Nichols, *Illustrations,* 2:90–91.

28. James Prior, *The Life of Edmond Malone* (London, 1860), p. 430. Cf. James L. Clifford, *From Puzzles to Portraits: Problems of a Literary Biographer* (Chapel Hill: University of North Carolina Press, 1970), p. 80: "The number of versions on one side [of an anecdote] need not be conclusive. They may all have come from a single unreliable source."

29. Stukeley's entry cannot be earlier than 1746, the year of Warburton's marriage and of his appointment to the preachership of Lincoln's Inn. For Stukeley's belief that "a change of fortune had chang'd [Warburton's] manners," see *Family Memoirs,* 1:129.

30. Ibid., pp. 128–29.

31. *The Divine Legation of Moses* (London, 1738), p. 183; Nadine Ollman, "William Warburton and Eighteenth-Century Criticism" (Ph.D. diss., University of Pennsylvania, 1971), p. 58; *Works,* 11:10.

32. *General Evening Post,* 12–14 December 1738, p. 1; *The History of the Works of the Learned,* December 1738, p. 425, and January 1739, p. 56. See also my "Another Defence by Warburton of the *Essay on Man,*" *Notes and Queries,* n.s. 26 (1979):24–25. It may be significant that a characteristic of first-born children is to suffer especially intense anxiety in times of stress and to seek relief by forming alliances. The year following the publication of the *Divine Legation* was unusually difficult for Warburton because of the attacks on the book's orthodoxy. The haste with which he rushed to Pope's defense, publishing two letters before he had even read the work he rebutted, suggests the possibility that he was also impelled by a craving for the security that a powerful literary ally might seem to confer. Cf. Stanley Schacter, *The Psychology of Affiliation: Experimental Studies of the Sources of Gregariousness* (Stanford: Stanford University Press, 1959), chaps. 5–6. Schacter shows that "anxiety produces considerably stronger manifestations of affiliative needs in first-born and only children than in later-born children" (p. 46).

33. Nichols, *Illustrations,* 2:53–54, 816; *Works,* 11:22.

34. Matthew Tindal's deist work *Christianity as Old as the Creation* (1730) alone elicited one hundred and fifty replies. See W. Neil, "The Criticism and Theological Use of the Bible, 1700–1950," in *The Cambridge History of the Bible: The West from the Reformation to the Present Day,* ed. S. L. Greenslade (Cambridge: Cambridge University Press, 1963), p. 243.

35. Advertisement to the first edition of *The Analogy of Religion* (1736) in *The Works of Joseph Butler,* ed. Samuel Halifax, 2 vols. (Edinburgh, 1817), 1:1ix–lx.

36. Sykes, *Edmund Gibson, Bishop of London, 1669–1748: A Study in Politics and Religion in the Eighteenth Century* (London: Oxford University Press, 1926), p. 244.

37. Brooke to Pope, [November 1739], in Pope's *Correspondence,* 4:199. Praise of Pope or the *Essay on Man* appears in the *Weekly Miscellany* for 12 May, 19 May, and 9 June 1733, 11 May 1734, and 10 May 1735. Of particular interest is a poem, "On Infidelity" by L. M. (19 May 1733, p. 3), containing the line *"But let* Pope's Numbers *check these haughty Foes,"* that is, of Christianity.

38. Hare to Warburton, 9 March 1737/8, in *A Selection from Unpublished Papers of William Warburton* (London, 1841), p. 102.

39. Nichols, *Illustrations,* 2:816.

40. Crousaz's errors and distortions are judiciously exposed by Samuel Johnson in the notes to his translation of the *Commentaire,* published as *A Commentary on Mr. Pope's Principles of Morality, or Essay on Man* (1739; reprint ed., New York: Garland, 1974).

41. White, *Pope and the Context of Controversy* (Chicago: University of Chicago Press, 1970), p. 11.

42. 24 February, 10 March, 24 March, 21 April, 28 April, 5 May, 12 May, 18 May, 26 May, 9 June, and 7 July 1738. The most substantial of these, with the addition of four published in 1739, are collected in *Remarks on the Divine Legation of Moses* (London, [1739]).

43. Notebook 1, letters 17, 23, 25–26, 34.

44. *Remarks on the Divine Legation,* pp. 27–28.

45. Conyers Middleton to Warburton, 5 August 1738, British Library add. MSS 32,457, f. 132.

46. Sykes, *Edmund Gibson* pp. 260–67; the *Weekly Miscellany,* 24 February and 24 March 1738.

47. January 1739, pp. 56–57.

48. *The Twickenham Edition of the Poems of Alexander Pope,* ed. John Butt, 10 vols. (New Haven: Yale University Press, 1939–67), vol. 3, pt. 1, *An Essay on Man,* ed. Maynard Mack (1950), p. xxi.

49. The word is "disconfictus." See Upton, *Critical Observations on Shakespeare,* p. li.

Chapter Two

1. My summary omits sections on sacrifice and miracles.

2. Passmore, *The Perfectibility of Man* (New York: Scribner's, 1970), p. 94n.

3. Ibid., p. 95.

4. Pearson, *A Critical Essay,* p. 50.

5. Rejecting the argument that God, being infinite, must offer infi-

nite rewards, Warburton remarks that "this reasoning holds equally on the side of the UNMERCIFUL DOCTORS, as they are called, who doom the Wicked to EVERLASTING PUNISHMENT" (*Works*, 6:253). The phrase "as they are called" seems to hedge.

6. Lovejoy, "The Parallel of Classicism and Deism," *Modern Philology* 29 (1932):281–99, reprinted in *Essays in the History of Ideas* (1948; reprint ed., New York: Braziller, 1955), p. 79.

7. 17 July 1767, in notebook 3, f. 132.

8. *The Prose Works of Jonathan Swift*, ed. Herbert Davis, 14 vols. (Oxford: Blackwell, 1939–68), vol. 2, *Bickerstaff Papers and Pamphlets on the Church* (1940), p. 7.

9. *Old Whig*, 13 and 27 May 1736.

10. *Weekly Miscellany*, 19 June 1736; *The Works . . . of Francis Blackburne* (Cambridge, 1805), pp. lx–x.

11. See, for instance, an attack on the contract theory in the *Weekly Miscellany*, 2 December 1737, in which "the *Infidel* State of *Nature* and *Independence*" is said to be "as chimerical, as it is wicked. . . ."

12. *Old Whig*, 27 May 1736, p. 2.

13. My discussion of the *Alliance* is everywhere indebted to Norman Sykes, *Church and State in England in the XVIIIth Century* (Cambridge, 1934), pp. 316–26.

14. Hans W. Frei, *The Eclipse of Biblical Narrative: A Study in Eighteenth and Nineteenth Century Hermeneutics* (New Haven: Yale University Press, 1974), pp. 52–53.

15. For a summary of Warburton's plan for the unwritten books, see *Works*, 6:234.

16. Devries, *The Mackeral Plaza* (Boston: Little, Brown, 1958), p. 8.

17. The argument is attributed to the deists in *Works*, 1:199; 6:234; 11:275.

18. See Leslie Stephen, *History of English Thought in the Eighteenth Century* 3d ed. (1902; reprint ed., New York, 1962), 1:302n.: "I must confess that I do not even know to what particular writings Warburton alludes in the main assumption. Certainly the point is not commonly urged by the deists whom he chiefly assails." Cf. John H. Overton and Frederic Relton, *The English Church from the Accession of George I to the End of the Eighteenth Century* (London: Macmillan & Co., 1906), p. 55; and W. R. S. Sorley, "Berkeley and Contemporary Philosophy," in *The Cambridge History of English Literature*, ed. A. W. Ward and A. R. Waller (1912; reprint ed., Cambridge: Cambridge University Press, 1962), 11:296. Though the deist Anthony Collins denied in a footnote that the ancient Jews believed in a future state, he did not conclude that the Pentateuch was therefore unworthy of God. He equated disbelief in immortality with freethinking, and since in his view freethinking was admirable, the ancient Jews were praise-

worthy to the extent that they disbelieved. See Collins's *A Discourse of Free-Thinking* (London: 1713), pp. 150–53.

19. Leland, *A View of the Principal Deistical Writers* . . . , 2 vols. (Edinburgh, 1807), 2:165–66.

20. It may be significant that with the third edition the phrase "on the Principles of a Religious Deist" was dropped from the title.

21. John Hick, *Death and Eternal Life* (New York: Harper, 1976), p. 62.

22. D. P. Walker, *The Decline of Hell: Seventeenth-Century Discussions of Eternal Torment* (Chicago: University of Chicago Press, 1964), pp. 69, 262.

23. Leland, *View of the Principal Deistical Writers*, 2:15–16.

24. G. E. Mylonas, *Eleusis and the Eleusinian Mysteries* (Princeton: Princeton University Press, 1961), pp. 282–84; S. G. F. Brandon, *The Judgment of the Dead: The Idea of Life After Death in the Major Religions* (New York: Scribner's, 1967), pp. 79–80.

25. Theobald to Warburton, 18 December 1731, in Jones, *Lewis Theobald*, p. 290.

26. Sterne, *Tristram Shandy*, ed. James Aiken Work (Indianapolis: Bobbs-Merrill, 1940), p. 610.

27. Emil G. Kraeling, *The Old Testament since the Reformation* (1955; reprint ed., New York: Schocken, 1969), p. 22; *Works* 5:441–42.

28. *Essays of the Late Mark Pattison*, ed. Henry Nettleship 2 vols. (Oxford, 1889), 2:167; T. W. Fowle, *The Divine Legation of Christ* (London, 1879), p. 4.

29. Arthur J. Lelyveld, "Future Life," in *The Universal Jewish Encyclopedia*, ed. Isaac Landman (New York: KTAV, 1969), 4:484–86; *The Interpreter's Bible*, ed. George Arthur Buttrick et al. (New York: Abingdon Press, 1956), 5:304.

30. Edmund F. Sutcliffe, *The Old Testament and the Future Life*, Bellarmine Series, no. 8 (London: Burns, Oates & Washbourne, 1946), p. 191.

31. Erik Iversen, *The Myth of Egypt and its Hieroglyphs in European Tradition* (Copenhagen: Gec Gad Publishers, 1961), pp. 103–5.

32. John David Wortham, *The Genesis of British Egyptology* (Norman: University of Oklahoma Press, 1971), pp. 42, 48.

33. Frank E. Manuel, *The Eighteenth Century Confronts the Gods* (Cambridge: Harvard University Press, 1959), p. 122; Clifton Cherpack, "Warburton and the Encyclopédie," *Comparative Literature* 7 (1955):226–39.

34. Cf. Sykes, *Edmund Gibson*, p. 241, and A. C. McGiffert, *Protestant Thought Before Kant* (1911; reprint ed., Gloucester, Mass.: Peter Smith, 1971), p. 243.

35. Herbert M. Morais, *Deism in Eighteenth Century America* (1934; reprint ed., New York: Russell & Russell, 1960), p. 104.

36. Leland, *View of the Principal Deistical Writers*, 1:71.

37. Albert J. Kuhn, "English Deism and the Development of Romantic Mythological Syncretism," *PMLA* 62 (1956):1111; Cherpack, "Warburton and the Encyclopédie"; J. H. Brumfitt, "Voltaire and Warburton," *Studies on Voltaire and the Eighteenth Century* 18 (1961):43–44.

38. Warburton to Philip Doddridge, 10 June 1749, in Nichols, *Illustrations,* 2:834.

39. The discrepancy between the subtitle and the text is the same in all editions.

40. Newman, *Two Essays,* 7th ed. (London, 1888), pp. 105–6.

Chapter Three

1. Joseph Spence, *Observations, Anecdotes, and Characters of Books and Men,* ed. James M. Osborn, 2 vols. (Oxford: Clarendon 1966), 1:217.

2. *The Works of Shakespear,* 8 vols. (London, 1747), 1:xviii–xix; hereafter cited in the text as *S.*

3. *The Works of Alexander Pope,* 9 vols. (London, 1751), 4:19–20n.; 1:189n.; hereafter cited in the text as *P.*

4. Warburton to Hurd, 17 May 1759, in *Prelate,* p. 285.

5. Review of Ruffhead's *Life of Pope, Gentleman's Magazine* 39 (1769):62.

6. *Eighteenth-Century Critical Essays,* ed. Scott Elledge, 2 vols. (Ithaca: Cornell University Press, 1961), 1:68–69, 62; *Shakespear,* 1:3n.; *Pope,* 1:139n.

7. See Ryley, "Warburton, Warton, and Ruffhead's *Life of Pope,*" *Papers on Language and Literature* 4 (1968):51–62.

8. Ruffhead, *Life of Pope* (London 1769), p. 439; Hurd, "A Dissertation on the Idea of Universal Poetry," in *Eighteenth-Century Critical Essays,* 2:860; *The Yale Edition of the Works of Samuel Johnson* (New Haven: Yale University Press, 1958–), vols. 7–8, *Johnson on Shakespeare,* ed. Arthur Sherbo, with introduction by Bertrand H. Bronson (1968), 7:67.

9. *Eighteenth-Century Critical Essays,* 1:67, 506, n. 133; Ruffhead, *Life of Pope,* p. 441. Cf. A. Bosker, *Literary Criticism in the Age of Johnson,* 2d ed. (Gronigen: J. B. Wolters, 1953), p. 217.

10. Ruffhead, *Life of Pope,* p. 440.

11. Ibid., pp. 440–41.

12. Evans, *Warburton,* pp. 205, 226, 262–66.

13. Ollman, "William Warburton and Eighteenth-Century Criticism" (Ph.D. diss., University of Pennsylvania, 1971), pp. 57–68, 96–145, 149–52.

14. John Milton, *Paradise Regained . . . To Which is Added Samson Agonistes: and Poems upon Several Occasions,* ed. Thomas Newton, 2 vols. (London, 1753), 2:121n.

15. René Wellek, *The Rise of English Literary History* (1941; reprint ed., New York: McGraw-Hill, 1966), p. 54.

16. *Shakespear*, vol. 2, unpaginated note following *Love's Labours Lost;* ibid., vol. 5, unpaginated note following *Richard III*.

17. Arthur Johnston, *Enchanted Ground: The Study of Medieval Romance in the Eighteenth Century* (London: University of London, Athlone Press, 1964), pp. 15, 18.

18. Warburton mistakes *Kyrie eleison de Montaubon,* the name of a character, for a title, and misunderstanding the Spanish word *romancero* ("ballad"), he wrongly supposes that *Roldan el encandado* (Warburton prints "el encantador") appears in a romance.

19. Edmond Malone, *Supplement to the Edition of Shakespeare's Plays Published in 1778,* 2 vols. (London, 1780), 1:373–80; Wellek, *Rise of English Literary History,* p. 153.

20. Malone, *Supplement,* 1:376, 379.

21. My quotations are from the facsimile reprint in *Prefaces to Fiction,* ed. Benjamin Boyce, Augustan Reprint Society Publications, no. 32 (Los Angeles: University of California, William Andrews Clark Memorial Library, 1952). Johnston, *Enchanted Ground,* p. 18, calls the essay an "abbreviated form" of the history of romance, but in fact it is a different work altogether.

22. Wellek, *Rise of English Literary History,* p. 150, writes that "the whole approach" of the note on drama "shows that a dim idea of an evolution of the genre was in his mind." The same might be said of the other histories as well.

23. This has been called one of the earliest sympathetic judgments of Gothic architecture. See Paul Frankl, *The Gothic: Literary Sources and Interpretations through Eight Centuries* (Princeton: Princeton University Press, 1960), pp. 391–92 and n.

24. Cf. E. D. Hirsch, Jr., "Carnal Knowledge," review of *The Genesis of Secrecy,* by Frank Kermode, in *New York Review of Books,* 14 June 1979, p. 18: "You can read through virtually all the major works of the important literary critics before the twentieth century without finding an extended discussion of the problem of interpretation. In Britain, writers like Sidney, Pope, Hume, Johnson, Coleridge, and Arnold simply did not question their interpretations of the texts they read. They asked of a piece of writing, 'Is it good?' or 'Why is it good?' rather than 'What does it mean?'

"By contrast, ever since the revolution begun by the New Critics during the 1940s, and the enormous increase in the numbers of academic interpreters over the past forty years, the question of value has fallen into the background and the question of interpretation has come to the fore."

25. Hurd acknowledges his indebtedness to the method of Warburton's commentary in the edition of Pope. See Hurd's edition of Horace,

Epistolae ad Pisones, et Augustum, 5th ed., 2 vols. (London, 1766), 1:xv–xvi; 2:iii. But the influence of the critical essays in the *Divine Legation* is also apparent and can be seen most vividly in Hurd's interpretation of Virgil's third Georgic in his Horace, 2:44–57. Cf. Stephen J. Curry, "The Literary Criticism of William Warburton," *English Studies* 48 (1967):35–48.

26. Peter Berek, "Interpretation, Allegory, and Allegoresis," *College English* 40 (1978):117–32. The quotation is on p. 118.

27. James Reeves, *The Reputation and Writings of Alexander Pope* (New York: Barnes and Noble, 1976), p. 227.

28. Some lines, Crousaz declares, "are altogether edifying in the mouth of an honest man, but . . . they give scandal and appear profane in the mouth of an ill one" (translated and quoted by Warburton, in *Works,* 11:57).

29. White, *Pope and the Context of Controversy,* p. 14.

30. Pope, *An Essay on Man,* ed. Maynard Mack, p. xxi.

31. "Critical Observations on the Design of the Sixth Book of the Aeneid," in *The English Essays of Edward Gibbon,* ed. Patricia B. Craddock (Oxford: Clarendon Press, 1972), p. 148. My two-part division of Warburton's essay is based on Gibbon, p. 134.

32. "Virgil and the Mystery Religions," *American Journal of Philology* 94 (1973):147–66. W. F. Jackson Knight praises Warburton's interpretation in "Cumaen Gates," in *Virgil: Epic and Anthropology,* ed. John D. Christie (New York: Barnes and Noble, 1967), p. 176.

33. R. F. Paget, *In the Footsteps of Orpheus* (London: Robert Hale, 1967), pp. 15, 73.

34. Sir Frank Fletcher, ed. *Aeneid VI* (1941; reprint ed., Oxford: Clarendon Press, 1972), pp. xiii–xiv.

35. Gibbon's pamphlet is the "Critical Observations" cited in note 31 above.

36. The critics with whom he argues are Addison (pp. 81–85, 135), St. Evremond (pp. 85–88), Blackwell (pp. 88–89), and Atterbury (pp. 167–68).

37. Hirsch, *Validity in Interpretation* (New Haven: Yale University Press, 1967), pp. 202–3.

38. "On Reading the Dissertation on the Sixth Book of Virgil," in Nichols, *Anecdotes,* 5:609–11n. Originally published in 1758, the poem consists of fifty-four lines in tetrameter couplets. Warburton's learning is said to be the golden bough that made possible his penetration of Virgil's mysteries.

39. *The Golden Ass,* trans. William Adlington, rev. by S. Gaselee, Leob Classical Library (Cambridge: Harvard University Press, 1915), pp. 507–37.

40. P. G. Walsh, *The Roman Novel* (Cambridge: Cambridge University Press, 1970), pp. 143, 186, 184, 220.

41. Ibid., p. 221, n. 4; Reinhold Merkelbach, *Roman und Mysterium in der Antike* (Munich: C. H. Beck'sche Verlagsbuchhandlung, 1962), p. 16.

42. J. Gwyn Griffiths, *Apuleius of Madaurus: The Isis Book (Metamorphosis, Book IX)* (Leiden: Brill, 1975), p. 28.

43. On the Warburton–Lowth controversy, see Evans, *Warburton,* pp. 247–55.

44. Lowth, *Lectures on the Sacred Poetry of the Hebrews,* trans. G. Gregory (London, 1847), p. 358 and n.

45. See Robert Gordis, *The Book of God and Man: A Study of Job* (Chicago: University of Chicago Press, 1965), p. 216.

46. Baly, *God and History in the Old Testament* (New York: Harper, 1976), p. 192. Baly concedes (p. 205n.) that his allegorical interpretation is not generally accepted.

47. Gordis, *Book of God,* pp. 15–18.

Chapter Four

1. Nichols, *Illustrations,* pp. 198, 204–656, 110; Jones, *Lewis Theobald,* pp. 264–345; Evans, *Warburton,* p. 151; Ronald Brunlees McKerrow, "The Treatment of Shakespeare's Text by His Earlier Editors, 1709–1768," *Proceedings of the British Academy* (1933), reprinted in *Ronald Brunlees McKerrow: A Selection of His Essays,* comp. John Phillip Imroth, Great Bibliographers Series, no. 1 (Metuchen, N.J.: Scarecrow Press, 1974), p. 180.

2. On the 1745 *Shakespear,* see Giles Dawson, "Warburton, Hanmer, and the 1745 Edition of Shakespeare," *Studies in Bibliography* 2 (1949–50):35–48, and Arthur Sherbo, "Warburton and the 1745 Shakespeare," *Journal of English and Germanic Philology* 51 (1952):71–82. Dawson and Sherbo disagree about the extent of Warburton's involvement in the 1745 edition. Support for Dawson's view that it must have been considerable is suggested by Warburton's handwritten notes in the printers' copy of *Henry VIII,* now in the Folger Shakespeare Library. On Warburton's revisions in his own copy of the *Shakespear,* see Norman Bennet, "Warburton's 'Shakespear,' " *Notes and Queries,* 8th ser. 3 (1893):141–42, 203, 262–63.

3. Warburton to Hurd, 31 January 1755, in *Prelate,* pp. 182–83.

4. I have not been able to find in Warburton's surviving correspondence a reference to his attending the performance of a play. Cf. *The Private Correspondence of David Garrick,* ed. James Boaden, 2 vols. (London, 1831), 1:63—"I cannot perceive, in any of Warburton's letters, that he attended his friend Garrick's theatre. Even to Hurd he abstains from all mention of his acting, and, at times, evinces a rather savage contempt for the stage. He thought, very obviously, that both Drs. Young and Brown, as clergymen, dishonoured themselves, by becoming dry-nurses to the theatre."

5. Pope, "Preface to *The Works of Shakespear"* and Theobald "Preface to *The Works of Shakespeare"* in *Eighteenth-Century Essays on Shakespeare,* ed.

David Nichol Smith, 2d ed. (Oxford: Clarendon Press, 1963), pp. 53, 74–75. On Theobald's three classes of editions, see McKerrow, "The Treatment of Shakespeare's Text," p. 187, n. 13.

6. Ronald B. McKerrow, *Prolegomena for the Oxford Shakespeare: A Study in Editorial Method* (Oxford: Clarendon Press, 1939), p. 36; "The Treatment of Shakespeare's Text," pp. 106–7.

7. *Milton's Paradise Lost* (London, 1732), p. 4. For a good discussion of Bentley's method and its influence, see Jones, *Lewis Theobald*, pp. 31–60.

8. Moyles, "Edward Capell (1713–1781) as Editor of *Paradise Lost*," *Transactions of the Cambridge Bibliographical Society* 6 (1975):255.

9. Not all editors acknowledged or defended their emendations. Rowe's, Pope's, and Hanmer's are silent.

10. *Milton's Paradise Lost*, sig. a2$^{r–v}$.

11. Alexander, "Restoring Shakespeare: The Modern Editor's Task," *Shakespeare Survey* 5 (1952):2. The phrase "door-keepers and prompters" is from Warburton's preface.

12. Though Warton moved poets from one class to another in the various editions of the *Essay*, he consistently retained a four-class division paralleling Warburton's. See Hoyt Trowbridge, "Joseph Warton's Classification of English Poets," *Modern Language Notes* 51 (1936):515–18.

13. Arthur Sherbo, *Samuel Johnson, Editor of Shakespeare, with an Essay on "The Adventurer*," Illinois Studies in Language and Literature, vol. 42 (Urbana: University of Illinois Press, 1956), pp. 51–52.

14. *Johnson on Shakespeare*, ed. Arthur Sherbo, 7:35–36.

15. Nicoll, "The Editors of Shakespeare from the First Folio to Malone," in *Studies in the First Folio* (London: Oxford University Press, 1924), p. 177.

16. Edwards's book, the first edition of which was entitled *A Supplement to Mr. Warburton's Edition of Shakespear*, went through seven editions between 1748 and 1765.

17. Quoted in John Hazel Smith, "Styan Thirlby's Shakespearean Commentaries: a Corrective Analysis," *Shakespeare Studies* 11 (1978):220, 234, and in Sherbo, *Samuel Johnson*, p. 43.

18. Jones, *Lewis Theobald*, p. 181.

19. Unless otherwise indicated, act, scene, and line numbers follow the Globe edition. See *Shakespear*, 2:338, n.7, and Benjamin Heath, *A Revisal of Shakespear's Text* (London, 1765), pp. 148–49.

20. This was the Reverend Charles Morton. See James Sutherland, *Defoe* (Philadelphia: Lippincott, 1938), pp. 22–23.

21. Greg, "Principles of Emendation in Shakespeare," in *Aspects of Shakespeare: Being British Academy Lectures* (Oxford: Clarendon Press, 1933), p. 130.

22. The first quotation in each pair follows the text of the Globe edition. Warburton's versions, in parentheses, appear in *Shakespear*, 1:342, n.

3; 2:266, n. 8; 2:329, n. 8; 2:239, n. 6; 3:11, n. 2; 3:34, n. 8; 7:290–91, n. 3.

23. T. R. Lounsbury, *The Text of Shakespeare: Its History from the Publication of the Quartos and Folios Down to and Including the Publication of the Editions of Pope and Theobald* (New York: Scribner's, 1906), pp. 508–9; *Shakespear,* 5:73, n. 3.

24. *The Works of Shakespeare* (London, 1733), 5:344, n. 17, Capell Collection, L. I–7, Library of Trinity College, Cambridge; *Shakespear,* 6:284–85, n. 2.

25. Smith, *Shakespeare in the Eighteenth Century* (Oxford: Clarendon Press, 1928), p. 44.

26. Theobald attributes emendations and glosses to Warburton and others who helped him with the edition, but he silently accepts textual changes made by Rowe and Pope.

27. Lounsbury, *The Text of Shakespeare,* p. 542.

28. Irene G. Dash, "A Glimpse of the Sublime in Warburton's Edition of *The Winter's Tale,*" *Shakespeare Studies* 11 (1978):170.

29. *Johnson on Shakespeare,* 8:973–74; *Shakespear,* 8:160–61, n. 1.

30. Theobald to Warburton, 8 April 1729, in Nichols, *Illustrations,* 2:209.

31. *Shakespear,* 8:166–67, n. 7; 1:399, n. 4; T. W. Baldwin, *William Shakespere's "Small Latine and Lesse Greeke,"* 2 vols. (1944; reprint ed., Urbana: University of Illinois Press, 1966), 2:526–27, 601–3.

32. Horace Howard Furness, ed., *A Midsummer Night's Dream* (1895; reprint ed., New York: Dover, 1963), pp. 75–91.

33. *Johnson on Shakespeare,* 8:975. For a discussion of the bibliographical implications of the two readings, see Fredson Bowers, "A Note on *Hamlet,* I.v.33 and II. ii.181," *Shakespeare Quarterly* 4 (1953):51–56.

34. Stockwell, "Shakespeare and the Dublin Pirates," *Dublin Magazine,* n.s. 4 (1929):25.

35. Pope's will in Ruffhead, *Life of Pope,* p. 546.

36. *The Works of Alexander Pope,* ed. Whitwell Elwin and William John Courthope, 10 vols. (1871–89; reprint ed., New York: Gordian Press, 1967), 3:92; *Twickenham Edition of the Poems of Alexander Pope,* vol. 3, pt. 2, *Epistles to Several Persons (Moral Essays),* ed. F. W. Bateson, 2d ed. (1961), pp. x–xiv.

37. Frank Brady, "The History and Structure of Pope's *To a Lady,*" *Studies in English Literature, 1500–1900* 9 (1969):450–51.

38. Pope, *Epistles,* p. xiii, n. 3.

39. Another reason may be the phrase "property of all . . . my works," a necessary circumlocution for copyright, since the term had not yet been coined. Earlier in the same paragraph, Pope leaves to Allen and Warburton his library of "printed books." When he means books, he says books.

40. In *Pope,* 1:iv–v, Warburton explains the delay in publication as

owing to his willingness to let Pope's beneficiaries profit from the sale of his unsold works. This explanation will not hold for the years after 1748, but, Brady's incredulity notwithstanding (p. 451), it is neither implausible for the earlier years nor inconsistent with Warburton's drawing the line at the sale of his own commentary for the benefit of the other heirs.

41. Pope, *Epistles,* p. xiv; *Twickenham Edition,* vol. 4, *Imitations of Horace,* ed. John Butt, 2d ed. (1961), pp. 93–94.

42. Pope, *Imitations,* pp. 93–94; Pope, *Epistles,* pp. 78–80.

43. R. H. Griffith, "Early Warburton? Or Late Warburton?" *University of Texas Studies in English* (1940), pp. 123–31.

44. *Monthly Review,* July 1751, pp. 101–2; *Pope,* 3:180n., 280n.; 4:36n.

45. *Pope,* 1:151n., 188–89n.; 5:287–88n.

46. Ibid., 4:101n.; 5:164–65n.; 4:306n.; Warburton to Middleton, 27 August 1738, British Library Egerton MSS 1953, f. 35.

47. Pope, *Epistles,* pp. 6–12.

48. *Poetical Works,* Oxford Standard Authors (London: Oxford University Press, 1966).

49. Smith, *Shakespeare in the Eighteenth Century,* p. 44.

50. Schmitz, *Pope's "Essay on Criticism" 1709* (St. Louis: Washington University Press, 1962), pp. 19–21.

51. *Twickenham Edition,* vol. 6, *Minor Poems,* ed. Norman Ault and John Butt (1954), pp. xiii, 223–25.

52. *The Correspondence of Alexander Pope,* 4:144, 234, 434, 455, 481.

53. Clifford, *From Puzzles to Portraits: Problems of a Literary Biographer* (Chapel Hill: University of North Carolina Press, 1970), p. 4.

54. Pope, *Imitations,* p. vi.

55. Gordis, *Book of God,* p. 17.

56. *The Sociology of Literary Taste,* trans. E. W. Dickes (London: Kegan Paul, 1944), p. 17.

57. Quoted in Douglas Grant, *James Thomson* (London: Cresset Books, 1951), p. 61.

58. Ibid., p. 276.

59. Pope, *Epistles,* p. 79.

60. *Twickenham Edition,* vol. 5, *The Dunciad,* ed. James Sutherland, 3d ed. (1963), pp. 308n., 442; Pope, *Epistles,* p. 100n.; Pope, *Imitations,* p. 298n. For Warburton's influence on the *Essay on Man,* see Robert W. Rogers, "Notes on Pope's Collaboration with Warburton in Preparing a Final Edition of the Essay on Man," *Philological Quarterly* 26 (1947):358–66; on the *Dunciad,* see Miriam Lerenbaum, *Alexander Pope's "Opus Magnum," 1729–1744* (Oxford: Clarendon Press, 1977), pp. 140–50.

61. Donald T. Siebert, Jr., introduction to *"A Letter to the Editor of the Letters on the Spirit of Patriotism, &c." and "A Familiar Epistle to the Most Im-*

pudent Man Living," Augustan Reprint Society Publication, no. 192 (Los Angeles: William Andrews Clark Memorial Library, 1978), p. ii.

62. 10 February 1749/50, in *Prelate,* p. 41.

63. Pope, *Works,* ed. Elwin and Courthope, 3:11; Pope, *Dunciad,* p. 83.

64. Pope, *Epistles,* p. 46n. For a similar example of ironic annotation by Warburton, see p. 86 below.

65. *Quarterly Review* 7 (1809):391–92; Evans, *Warburton,* pp. 148–55, and see below, pp. 98–100.

66. Courthope, "Pope, the Byzantine Empress, and Walpole's Whore," *Review of English Studies,* n.s. 6 (1955):372–82; Pope, *Works,* ed. Elwin and Courthope, 3:13.

67. Pope, *Works,* ed. Elwin and Courthope, 3:533.

68. From the beginning, the poem was printed in the prologue position, a place it had never before held in Pope's works, suggesting that the idea of a prologue had been in Warburton's mind long before he either wrote or canceled the note on Mallet.

Chapter Five

1. Crossley, "The Literary Characters of Bishop Warburton and Dr. Johnson," p. 249.

2. *Lives of the English Poets,* ed. George Birkbeck Hill, 3 vols. (1905; reprint ed., New York: Octagon, 1967), 3:166.

3. Bodleian Library MS English Letters d. 35, ff. 34v, 52. 48v; Nichols, *Illustrations,* pp. 44, 28, 46; Boston Public Library MS ch. g. 12.57, and *Prelate,* pp. 441–43.

4. Malone to Percy, 21 March 1809, in *The Percy Letters,* vol. 1, *The Correspondence of Thomas Percy and Edmond Malone,* ed. Arthur Tillotson (1944; reprint ed., New Haven: Yale University Press, 1960), p. 249.

5. Nichols, *Anecdotes,* 5:652; William Seward, *Anecdotes of Some Distinguished Persons* (London, 1797), 5:165.

6. 29 May 1758, quoted in *Selected Letters of Samuel Richardson,* ed. John Carrol (Oxford: Clarendon Press, 1964), p. 17; Warburton to Hurd, 17 May 1759, in *Prelate,* p. 285.

7. *North Country Diaries,* 2d ser., Publications of the Surtees Society, no. 124 (Durham: Surtees Society, 1915), pp. 196–98; Joseph Spence, *Observations, Anecdotes and Characters of Books and Men,* ed. James M. Osborn, 2 vols. (Oxford: Clarendon Press, 1966), 1:951. Cf. Robert M. Ryley, "The Identity of the 'Fo-ol' in Spence's Anecdotes," *Notes and Queries* 24 (1977):264–65.

8. Warburton to Balguy, 10 May 1772, in Notebook 3, ff. 173–74. Kippis is quoted by Evans, *Warburton,* p. 272.

9. Warburton to Taylor, [December 1739], in Notebook 1, f. 66; to Ralph Allen, 26 November 1763, in Kilvert, *Selection,* p. 232.

10. [July 1775], in Notebook 3, f. 188; 20 January 1751/2, in Notebook 2, letter 9. Pages in Notebook 2 are unnumbered.

11. To Taylor, 15 May 1740, in Notebook 1, f. 103; to Doddridge, 2 February 1740/1, in Nichols, *Illustrations,* pp. 823–24.

12. *The Complete Works of William Hazlitt,* ed. P. P. Howe, 21 vols. (1932; reprint ed., New York: AMS Press, 1967), 11:222.

13. To Hurd, 30 January 1759, in *Prelate,* p. 277.

14. John Mitford's extracts from Warburton's letters to Mason, British Library add. MSS 32,563, f. 21.

15. To Taylor, 30 January 1730/1, in Notebook 1, f. 24; to Balguy, 8 January 1759 and 11 February 1758, in Notebook 3, ff. 81, 68; to the Reverend John Andrews, 25 March 1763, in Watson, *Life,* p. 548; to Balguy, 5 July 1769, 7 February 1768, in Notebook 3, ff. 150, 141v; to Balguy, 24 March 1751/2, in Notebook 2, letter 11; to Taylor, 27 November 1740, in Notebook 1, f. 108; to Balguy, 1756, in Notebook 3, ff. 49–50; to Taylor, 29 November 1731, in Notebook 1, f. 42; Mitford's extracts from letters to Mason, British Library add. MSS 32,563, f. 28.

16. 7 September 1737, in Nichols, *Illustrations,* p. 47 and n.

17. *The Private Correspondence of David Garrick,* 2 vols. (London, 1831), 1:63n.

18. Evans, *Warburton,* pp. 148–55.

19. Pierpont Morgan Library MS R–V Autographs, bishops of England.

20. Quoted in James Boswell, *Life of Johnson,* ed. George Birkbeck Hill and L. F. Powell (1934; reprint ed., Oxford: Clarendon, 1971), 1:263.

21. Sherlock to Warburton, 10 May 1739, in Kilvert, *Selection,* pp. 84–85.

22. Warburton to Thomas Birch, 10 September 1739, in Nichols, *Illustrations,* p. 110.

23. To Mrs. Thrale, 27 October 1777, cited by Howard Anderson and Irvin Ehrenpreis, "The Familiar Letter in the Eighteenth-Century: Some Generalizations," in *The Familiar Letter in the Eighteenth Century,* ed. Howard Anderson, Philip B. Daghlian, and Irvin Ehrenpreis (1966; reprint ed., Lawrence: University Press of Kansas, 1968), pp. 272–73.

24. For slighting references to Stukeley, see Nichols, *Illustrations,* p. 827; to Thomas Birch, *Prelate,* p. 126; to Hurd, British Library add. MSS 32,563, f. 21.

25. 17 December 1763, in Notebook 3, f. 111.

26. *Johnson on Shakespeare,* 7:xxxviii and n., 13n. It must be added that Warburton complained of Johnson's "insolence," "folly," and "malignity" (*Prelate,* p. 367n.).

Chapter Six

1. Evans, *Warburton,* p. 281; John Disney, *Memoirs of the Life and Writings of Arthur Ashley Sykes* (London, 1785), p. 269.

2. Jesse Appleton, *A Sermon, Delivered at Brunswick, April 13, 1815 . . .* (Hallowel, Me., 1815), pp. 18–19n.; Thomas Turton, *Natural Theology Considered with Reference to Lord Brougham's Discourse on that Subject* (Cambridge, 1836), p. 298.

3. Fowle, *The Divine Legation of Christ,* p. 1.

4. *Essays on the Late Mark Pattison,* 2:119–76; Stephen, *English Thought,* 1:292–315.

5. James L. Clifford and Donald J. Greene, *Samuel Johnson: A Survey and Bibliography of Critical Studies* (Minneapolis: University of Minnesota Press, 1970), p. 7.

6. Pattison, "Tendencies of Religious Thought in England, 1688–1750," in *Essays and Reviews,* 8th ed. (London, 1861), p. 264; Pattison, *Essays,* 2:157.

7. MacDonald, *Pope and His Critics: A Study in Eighteenth Century Personalities* (London: Dent, 1951), pp. 230, 322; *The Penguin Companion to English Literature,* ed. David Daiches (New York: McGraw-Hill, 1971), p. 541.

8. *Verses Occasioned by Mr. Warburton's Late Edition of Mr. Pope's Works* (London, 1751), pp. 13–14.

9. Pattison's review in the *British Quarterly Review* 55 (1872):219–36, is reprinted in *Essays,* 2:350–95. See also *Fraser's Magazine,* n.s. 3 (1871):284–301; *Quarterly Review* 143 (1872):321–61.

10. Lerenbaum, *Alexander Pope's "Opus Magnum,"* p. ix.

11. Harold J. Laski, *Political Thought in England: Locke to Bentham* (London: Oxford University Press, 1920), p. 80. See also the essay by R. W. Greaves cited in the Bibliography below.

12. The eighteenth-century French translation of Warburton's essay on hieroglyphics has recently been reprinted with a preface by Derrida. See Warburton, *Essai sur les hiéroglyphes des Égyptiens,* trans. Léonard des Malpeines, ed. Patrick Tort, preceded by "Scribble (pouvoir/écrire)" by Jacques Derrida, and "Transfigurations (archéologie du symbolique)" by Patrick Tort, Collection Palimpseste (Paris: Aubier Flammarion, 1977).

Selected Bibliography

PRIMARY SOURCES

1. Collected Works

The Works of the Right Reverend William Warburton, D.D., Lord Bishop of Gloucester: A New Edition . . . to which is prefixed A Discourse by Way of General Preface; Containing Some Account of the Life, Writings, and Character of the Author; by Richard Hurd, D.D., Lord Bishop of Worcester. 12 vols. London: T. Cadell & W. Davies, 1811.

2. Individual Works in Full or in Part by Warburton

The Alliance between Church and State, or, The Necessity and Equity of an Established Religion and a Test-law demonstrated, from the Essence and End of Civil Society, upon the fundamental Principles of the Law of Nature and Nations. In Three Parts. London: F. Gyles, 1736.

A Critical and Philosophical Commentary on Mr. Pope's Essay on Man: In which is contain'd A Vindication of the said Essay from the Misrepresentations of Mr. De Resnel, the French Translator, and of Mr. De Crousaz, Professor of Philosophy and Mathematics in the Academy of Lausanne, the Commentator. London: J. & P. Knapton, 1742.

A Critical and Philosophical Inquiry into the Causes of Prodigies and Miracles, as related by Historians. With an Essay towards restoring a Method and Purity in History. 2 parts. London: T. Corbett, 1727.

The Divine Legation of Moses demonstrated, on the Principles of a Religious Deist, from the Omission of the Doctrine of a Future State of Reward and Punishment in the Jewish Dispensation: In Six Books. 2 vols. London: F. Gyles, 1738–41.

The Doctrine of Grace; or, The Office and Operations of the Holy Spirit vindicated from the Insults of Infidelity and the Abuses of Fanaticism. 2 vols. London: A. Millar & J. & R. Tonson, 1763.

Julian, or A Discourse Concerning the Earthquake and Fiery Eruption, which defeated the Emperor's Attempt to rebuild the Temple at Jerusalem: In which The Reality of a Divine Interposition is shewn; The Objections to it are answered; and The Nature of that Evidence which demands the assent of every reasonable man to a Miraculous fact, is considered and explained. London: J. & P. Knapton, 1750.

Letters from a Late Eminent Prelate to One of His Friends. 2d ed. London: T. Cadell & W. Davies, 1809.

Letters from the Reverend Dr. Warburton, Bishop of Gloucester, to the Hon. Charles Yorke, from 1752 to 1770. London: Philanthropic Society, 1812.

The Life of Alexander Pope, Esq. Compiled from Original Manuscripts; with a Critical Essay on his Writings and Genius. By Owen Ruffhead, Esq. London: C. Bathurst, &c., 1769. Written under Warburton's direction and partially revised by him.

Miscellaneous Translations, in Prose and Verse, from Roman Poets, Orators, and Historians. London: A. Barker, 1724.

The Principles of Natural and Revealed Religion occasionally opened and explained; In a Course of Sermons preached before the Honourable Society of Lincoln's Inn. 2 vols. London: J. & P. Knapton, 1753–54.

Remarks on Mr. David Hume's Essay on the Natural History of Religion: Addressed to the Rev. Dr. Warburton. London: M. Cooper, 1757. Compiled by Richard Hurd from Warburton's marginal comments on Hume's book.

A Selection from Unpublished Papers of the Right Reverend William Warburton, D.D., late Lord Bishop of Gloucester. By the Reverend Francis Kilvert. London: J. B. Nichols and Son, 1841.

Sermons and Discourses on Various Subjects and Occasions. London: J. & R. Tonson, & A. Millar, 1767. Uniform with vols. 1–2 of *The Principles of Natural and Revealed Religion* and intended as vol. 3 of that work.

A View of Lord Bolingbroke's Philosophy, Compleat, in Four Letters to a Friend: In which the Whole System of Infidelity and Naturalism is Exposed and Confuted. 2d ed. London: J. & R. Tonson, 1756.

3. Works Edited by Warburton

The Works of Shakespear: . . . The Genuine Text (Collated with all the former Editions, and then corrected and emended) is here settled: Being restored from the Blunders of the first Editors, and the Interpolations of the two Last: With a Comment and Notes, Critical and Explanatory. By Mr. Pope and Mr. Warburton. 8 vols. London: J. & P. Knapton, &c., 1747.

The Works of Alexander Pope Esq. . . . With His Last Corrections, Additions, and Improvements; As they were delivered to the Editor a little before his Death: Together With The Commentaries and Notes of Mr. Warburton. 9 vols. London: J. & P. Knapton, H. Lintot, J. & R. Tonson, & S. Draper, 1751.

4. Unpublished Materials

Austin, Texas. University of Texas. Harry Ransom Center. Warburton papers. Transcripts in various hands of 50 letters to Robert Taylor and 121 letters to Thomas Balguy. The largest single collection of unpublished letters.

SECONDARY SOURCES

Boyce, Benjamin. *The Benevolent Man: A Life of Ralph Allen of Bath.*
Cambridge, Mass.: Harvard University Press, 1967. Contains
important information about Warburton's relations with the Allen
family. Attributes to Warburton the pamphlet *A Letter to
Mr. Archibald Cleland* (1744).

Brumfitt, J. H. "Voltaire and Warburton." *Studies on Voltaire and the
Eighteenth Century* 18 (1961):35–56. Traces Voltaire's changing
attitudes toward Warburton and Warburton's toward Voltaire. Points
out Voltaire's many borrowings from the *Divine Legation,* especially in
the *Philosophie de l'histoire.*

Cherpack, Clifton. "Warburton and the Encyclopédie." *Comparative
Literature* 7 (1955):226–39. Shows that at least twenty-three articles
in the *Encyclopédie* were lifted, most without acknowledgment, from
the *Alliance between Church and State* and the *Divine Legation.*

————— . "Warburton and Some Aspects of the Search for the Primitive in
Eighteenth-Century France." *Philological Quarterly* 36 (1957):221–33.
Ideas on the primitive in Rousseau and Monboddo can be traced back
through Condillac to Warburton.

Croswell, Andrew. *Observations on Several Passages in a Sermon Preached by
William Warburton, Lord Bishop of Gloucester, Before the Society for
propagating the Gospel in Foreign Parts: On Friday February 21, 1766.
Wherein Our Colonies are defended against his most injurious and abusive
Reflections.* Boston: Thomas & John Fleet, 1768. The only self-
contained work on Warburton published in America before the
present book. Besides attacking, probably with justice, Warburton's
ignorance of religious conditions in the colonies, Croswell complains
that his pulpit style is insufficiently grave and that he does not
believe in the necessity of grace for salvation.

Curry, Stephen J. "The Literary Criticism of William Warburton."
English Studies 48 (1967):35–48. Discusses the history of romance and
the essay on Virgil, emphasizing the originality and influence of
Warburton's use of history to explain literary form and interpret
meaning.

Dash, Irene G. "A Glimpse of the Sublime in Warburton's Edition of *The
Winter's Tale.*" *Shakespeare Studies* 11 (1978):159–74. A respectful
discussion of Warburton's commentary on the play, stressing his
interest in the sublime and the picturesque.

Doherty, F. M. "Sterne and Warburton: Another Look." *British Journal
for Eighteenth-Century Studies* 1 (1978):20–30. Argues that the *Divine
Legation* may have been a significant influence on *Tristram Shandy* and
that Sterne probably admired Warburton more than has been realized.

Evans, A. W. *Warburton and the Warburtonians: A Study in Some Eighteenth-Century Controversies.* London: Oxford University Press, 1932. The standard biography and indispensable. Contains a reasonably complete Warburton bibliography, though his contributions to newspapers and journals are not listed and the section on Warburtonian controversies lacks several important titles.

Greaves, R. W. "The Working of the Alliance: A Comment on Warburton." In *Essays in Modern English Church History in Memory of Norman Sykes,* edited by G. V. Bennett and J. D. Walsh. New York: Oxford University Press, 1966. Analyzes the *Alliance between Church and State* as "one of the most remarkable and influential books of the century."

Jones, Richard Foster. *Lewis Theobald: His Contribution to English Scholarship, with Some Unpublished Letters.* 1919. Reprint. New York: AMS Press, 1966. The best account of the eighteenth-century craze for conjectural emendation. Contains letters from Theobald to Warburton.

Luck, George. "Virgil and the Mystery Religions." *American Journal of Philology* 94 (1973):147–66. Argues that Warburton was essentially correct about the role of the Eleusinian Mysteries in *Aeneid,* book 6.

New, Melvin. "Sterne, Warburton, and the Burden of Exuberant Wit." *Eighteenth-Century Studies* 15 (1982):245–74. Advances a rather Warburtonian paradox—that Warburton symbolized for Sterne both artistic inhibition and intellectual fecundity. Discovers a number of heretofore undetected allusions to Warburton in *Tristram Shandy.*

Nichols, John. *Illustrations of the Literary History of the Eighteenth Century: Consisting of Authentic Memoirs and Original Letters of Eminent Persons, and Intended as a Sequel to the Literary Anecdotes.* 8 vols. London: Nichols & Bentley, 1817–58. Most of volume 2 is devoted to Warburton's correspondence with various friends. Occasional Warburtoniana appears in other volumes.

————. *Literary Anecdotes of the Eighteenth Century; Comprizing Biographical Memoirs of William Bowyer, F.S.A., and Many of His Friends.* 9 vols. London: Nichols & Bentley, 1812–16. A life of Warburton in volume 5 is not always reliable but contains much curious information and many letters. Occasional Warburtoniana appears in other volumes.

Pearson, John Norman. *A Critical Essay on the Ninth Book of Bishop Warburton's Divine Legation of Moses: Published in consequence of having gained the Annual Prize, Instituted by the late Rev. J. Hulse, A. M. of St. John's College.* Cambridge: Deighton, 1808. Evidently the only published study of book 9 of the *Divine Legation.* Takes issue with Warburton on almost every point of doctrine but praises his learning and intellect.

R., C. [James Crossley]. "On the Literary Characters of Bishop

Warburton and Dr. Johnson." *Blackwood's Edinburgh Magazine* 8 (1820):243–52. Chiefly interesting as evidence of Warburton's still-lofty reputation, though probably few besides Crossley would have ranked him with Johnson even then.

Rogers, Robert W. *The Major Satires of Alexander Pope.* Illinois Studies in Language and Literature, vol. 40. Urbana: University of Illinois Press. Chapter 5 is a thorough discussion of the Pope–Warburton friendship and of their collaboration on the *Essay on Criticism,* the *Essay on Man,* the *Moral Essays,* and the *Dunciad.*

Ryley, Robert M. "Warburton, Warton, and Ruffhead's *Life of Pope.*" *Papers on Language and Literature* 4 (1968):51–62. Tries to determine the extent of Warburton's collaboration in the writing of the *Life* by studying his corrections in the proof sheets. Wrongly supposes that when a correction fails to appear in the published text, Ruffhead "refused" to accept it. In fact, considerations of cost probably limited the number of cancels. The author was also unaware when he wrote the article that Ruffhead had theorized about biography in reviews published in the early 1760s—a probable factor in Warburton's choosing him to write the book.

Stephen, Sir Leslie. *History of English Thought in the Eighteenth Century.* 3d ed. 2 vols. 1902. Reprint, with a new preface by Crane Brinton. New York: Harcourt, Brace & World, 1962. The discussion of Warburton in volume 1 is among the most hostile ever written.

Sykes, Norman. *Church and State in England in the XVIIIth Century.* Cambridge: Cambridge University Press, 1934. Essential for an understanding of the Church of England in the eighteenth century.

Templeman, William Darby. "Warburton and Brown Continue the Battle Over Ridicule." *Huntington Library Quarterly* 17 (1953):17–36. The best account of Warburton's discovery of John "Estimate" Brown, who took Warburton's side in the controversy over Shaftesbury's notion that ridicule is a test of truth. Prints for the first time Warburton's initial letter to Brown.

Watson, John Selby. *The Life of William Warburton, D.D., Lord Bishop of Gloucester, from 1760 to 1779: with Remarks on His Works.* London: Longman, Green, Longman, Robert, & Green, 1863. Dutiful, uninspired, and based entirely on published sources. Superseded by Evans but useful for an occasional detail and for clear summaries of the theological works.

[Whitaker, Thomas Dunham.] Review of *The Works of William Warburton* (1811). *Quarterly Review* 7 (1812):383–407. A brilliant essay. Overpraises Warburton but with a clear-eyed recognition of his faults.

Index

DATE DUE

DEMCO 38-297